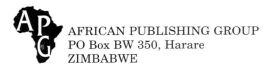

AFRICAN PUBLISHING GROUP
PO Box BW 350, Harare
ZIMBABWE

© David Martin. Pictures as credited, maps and published edition APG

Photographic credits: Tony Martin, cover 17 and 21; Maps by Surveyor General of Zimbabwe; National Archives of Zimbabwe, 7, 13, 39, 41, 43, 44, 79 and 84; Shearwater Adventures, 15, 59, 60 63 and back cover; Nick Greaves, 26, 70 and 73; Dirk Heinrich, 31; Steve Bolnick, 32, 33, 36 and 83; Dusty Durrant, 46; United Touring, 61; Elephant Hills, 66; Glynn's Holdings, 79; remainder David Martin.

ISBN: 1-77901-136-9

First printed 1997
Reprinted 1999

Design: Paul Wade, Ink Spots, Harare

Printed by: Cannon Press, Harare

# CONTENTS

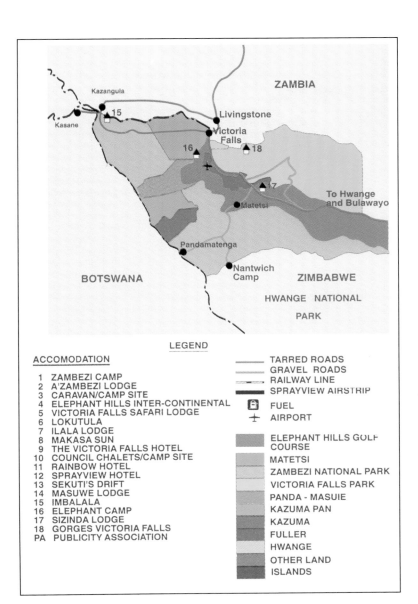

## LEGEND

### ACCOMODATION

1 ZAMBEZI CAMP
2 A'ZAMBEZI LODGE
3 CARAVAN/CAMP SITE
4 ELEPHANT HILLS INTER-CONTINENTAL
5 VICTORIA FALLS SAFARI LODGE
6 LOKUTULA
7 ILALA LODGE
8 MAKASA SUN
9 THE VICTORIA FALLS HOTEL
10 COUNCIL CHALETS/CAMP SITE
11 RAINBOW HOTEL
12 SPRAYVIEW HOTEL
13 SEKUTI'S DRIFT
14 MASUWE LODGE
15 IMBALALA
16 ELEPHANT CAMP
17 SIZINDA LODGE
18 GORGES VICTORIA FALLS
PA PUBLICITY ASSOCIATION

TARRED ROADS
GRAVEL ROADS
RAILWAY LINE
SPRAYVIEW AIRSTRIP
FUEL
AIRPORT

ELEPHANT HILLS GOLF COURSE
MATETSI
ZAMBEZI NATIONAL PARK
VICTORIA FALLS PARK
PANDA - MASUIE
KAZUMA PAN
KAZUMA
FULLER
HWANGE
OTHER LAND
ISLANDS

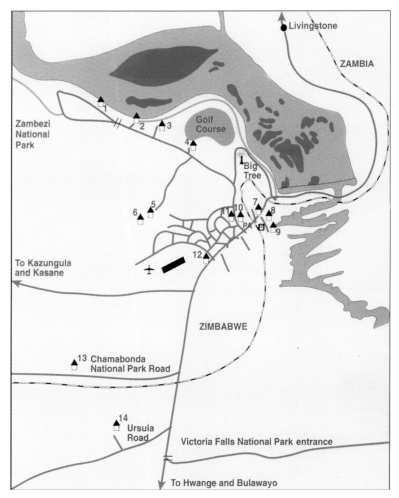

Livingstone

ZAMBIA

1

Zambezi
National
Park

2
3

Golf
Course

4

Big
Tree

6 5

11 10 7
8

PA

9

12

To Kazungula
and Kasane

ZIMBABWE

13 Chamabonda
National Park Road

14
Ursula
Road

Victoria Falls National Park entrance

To Hwange and Bulawayo

# V I C T O R I A
# F A L L S

## ACKNOWLEDGMENTS

Innumerable people over the past 40 years have provided me with personal and contrasting insights during my many visits to Victoria Falls.

Yet, it was not until I began to write this Guide, that I realised just how little I really knew about Victoria Falls and all the forces and factors that had contributed to moulding it.

The geology proved particularly interesting and I am grateful to Kevin Walsh of the University of Zimbabwe, Department of Geology, for arousing my interest and guiding me.

The walk with Dr Kit Hustler along the banks of the Zambezi River provided insights into the avian world and Meg Coates-Palgrave's expertise separated the trees from the shrubs.

Kathleen Ginn and David Mupfurutsa of African Publishing Group gave invaluable support, and Judy Boyd copy edited the manuscript. The Victoria Falls Safari Lodge and The Victoria Falls Hotel provided hospitality, as did Southern Cross Aviation, Shearwater, Frontiers Adventures and Avis.

Finally I must thank my companion and friend, Phyllis Johnson, who I met at Victoria Falls, for her support, encouragement, and comments on the manuscript.

## INTO AFRICA TRAVEL GUIDES

This is the fifth area-specific Guide to Zimbabwe. Others in the series published to date cover Bvumba, Great Zimbabwe, Hwange and Kariba. Guides on Harare and Bulawayo/Matobo will soon follow.

Most of the Guides follow a basic pattern. They begin with geology, followed by archaeology, which allows coverage of the Stone Age. The Iron Age is covered in the pre-colonial section, then the colonial period follows. Thereafter, specific attractions for each area are detailed.

In these Guides I am endeavouring to take the visitor beyond the pretty pictures and adjectives normally associated with travel literature. It is my hope that this Guide for you, like myself, will prove informative, opening up new panoramas.

David Martin

# INTRODUCTION

Recollections of my first visit to Victoria Falls in 1958 are somewhat hazy. In part this is due to the passing of time. In larger measure it is because I was distracted by the beauty of a leading British model of the day.

But such recollections as I have are of a "Blimpish" place frequented by retired British army officers, tweeded and brogued ladies, wealthy American and European tourists, and the few, mostly South African whites, who could afford to stay in the only hotel, or who camped.

It was certainly far removed from today's "rainbow", mass-market, tourism which is now so conspicuous at Victoria Falls.

The Bulawayo to Victoria Falls road was "strip" in those days. This consisted of two narrow strips of tar upon which one endeavoured to drive. When the occasional car approached or you had to overtake another vehicle, you navigated uneasily, two wheels on the tar, the other two in the sand.

A 1950 picture of cars on the old strip road.

My father had visited Victoria Falls in about 1930. He was for most of the time a "gentleman's gentleman" to a typical "Blimp", a much decorated, retired cavalry Colonel who had been born into great wealth in a titled family and who devoted his energies to such pursuits as visiting Victoria Falls.

7

Upon reflection I doubt a great deal had changed between 1930 and 1958. Possibly the strips were new, but not much else would have been.

Dr David Livingstone had seen the Falls in November 1855. Once it was said he had "discovered" them. That is now accepted as incorrect. Late Stone Age groups had preceded him by at least 100 centuries, our earliest ancestors by at least two million years.

As it came to be accepted that Livingstone had not "discovered" Victoria Falls it was claimed that he was the first white man to see them.

Such a claim pre-supposes that for a white man – as opposed to a black man or a woman of either hue – to see the Falls is of added significance. Beyond the obviously racist and sexist (not to mention irrelevant) connotation of such a statement, there is also a question mark as to whether Livingstone was indeed the first white man to see the Falls.

Several others, including British author William Cooley, Portuguese slave-and-ivory trader silva Antonio Francisco Porto, and a Hungarian, Ladislaus Magyar, may all have preceded Livingstone.

A statue of Dr David Livingstone, moon behind, looks across Victoria Falls from the Devils Cataract towards Zambia.

What can be said with certainty is that Livingstone publicised the Falls – and himself – in Europe in a way in which no one had previously done.

A further thing that can be said of Livingstone is that he named Victoria Falls after the British Queen of the day (Queen Victoria) and that name is still widely used today.

Immediately prior to Livingstone's arrival, the Falls had been called *Mosi-oa-Tunya*, meaning the Smoke that Thunders, by the ruling Kololo people on the northern bank. The Nambya people on the southern bank called them, as they still do today, *Chinotimba,* the Place that Thunders. Chinotimba is now the name of Victoria Falls' predominantly African township.

The Zezuru call them *Mapopoma* which imitates the sound they make. The Matabele today often call them *Amapopoma efolosi* meaning a waterfall at a place called Falls. Queen Victoria does not merit a mention in any local language!

*Mosi-oa-Tunya* had only been in usage for about 17 years before Livingstone's arrival. The name followed the overthrow of the ruling Lozi by the Kololo who were related to the Zulus and who had travelled north into the area from South Africa.

---

### Victoria Falls

Width 1,708 metres (5,604 feet).
Depth at highest point 103 metres (338 feet).
Volume of water 500 million litres (17.6 million cubic feet) a minute in full flood.

Victoria Falls publicity describes it as "the largest curtain of falling water in the world." At 10.8 km Khone Falls in Laos is the world's widest. But this is broken by many islands. The highest are Angel Falls (locally known as Churun-Meru) in Venezuela.

Iguaìra Falls on the border between Brazil and Paraguay used to have the highest water flow rate. But a dam has decreased this and now the highest flow rate is held by Buyoma Falls (formerly Stanley Falls) in Congo (formerly Zaire).

Viewed from the Zimbabwean bank of the Zambezi River, the Devil's Cataract is the first part of Victoria Falls. Then comes Cataract Island, the Main Falls, Rainbow Falls, and Eastern Cataract on the Zambian side.

---

Until 1838, according to Livingstone, the Falls had been known as *Shongwe.* But current historians doubt the veracity of Livingstone's claim, believing he was confused having just passed through the Shangwe area.

Of greater importance than the name is the history of the Zambezi River, the Falls themselves, the people who once lived in the area, and the threat the Falls now faces.

The Zambezi River as we know it today was originally two rivers. The Upper Zambezi from its source flowed into what was Lake Makgadikgadi in Botswana. The Middle (now Lake Kariba), and Lower Zambezi, flowing through Mozambique to the Indian Ocean, formed a separate river.

Lake Makgadikgadi was fed by the Okavango and Chobe Rivers and local rainfall; the evaporation off-take was replenished by the waters of what we now know as the Upper Zambezi River. The lake covered an area of roughly 60,000 square km and its eastern edge was a mere 65 metres west of the lip of today's Victoria Falls.

What then followed is known by geologists as "river capture" with the Middle Zambezi "capturing" its upper tributaries.

Global warming, a phrase in wide usage today, appears to have caused Lake Makgadikgadi to overflow in the interglacial period which preceded the last Ice Age some 125,000 to 150,000 years ago.

Scientific analysis of sediments and other remains show that when Lake Makgadikgdi overflowed, global temperatures averaged two degrees centigrade warmer than today.

As a result, Lake Makgadikgadi spilled onto the basalt plateau. The volume of water then gouged its way through cracks filled with softer materials joining up with the Middle Zambezi to create one river system. Lake Makgadikgadi, formally known by geologists as Greater palaeo-lake Makgadikgadi, dried up and today appears on the map as a pan in Botswana, southwest of Hwange.

The first Victoria Falls were created some time after the cataclysmic flood that saw the birth of the Zambezi River as we now know it.

But those Falls were located downstream of today's Victoria Falls at the

The Devils Cataract, possible site of the next Victoria Falls, in flood.

first of the eight gorges in Batoka Gorge. Since then the river has slowly, but inexorably, been cutting backwards, exposing one weakness after another in the basalt base and creating the zigzag pattern of gorges visible from the air.

The Sangoan people would have witnessed that river capture, the unification of the Zambezi River, and the creation of the first Victoria Falls. Today, imperceptibly, we are witnessing new changes in the line of the river and location of the Falls.

The people who lived along the river, their basic "tool kit", habits and diet, are covered in the archaeological section. Thereafter, Victoria Falls today is dealt with, including the recent very rapid evolution of human development at the Falls which raises grave concern.

Visitors arriving at Victoria Falls airport.

The strip road has gone. In its place is a new highway along which cars and luxury buses speed. At Victoria Falls Airport, aeroplanes from several regional destinations disgorge tourists into waiting zebra-striped buses and four-wheel-drive vehicles. At least one major European airline is trying to get landing rights.

On the Zambezi River, "booze cruise" boats, canoes, rubber dinghies and all manner of craft ply the waters. Overhead, helicopters, float and fixed-wing planes (exceeding acceptable noise pollution levels), microlights and ultralights, together all make around 150 flights daily.

Until 1960, Victoria Falls had only one hotel, The Victoria Falls Hotel, opened in 1904 with 16 bedrooms. Then the local council built a rest camp. Tourist visits remained manageable with only a few thousand able to afford the time and expense involved in a visit to the Falls.

When The Victoria Falls Hotel opened its doors in June 1904 the all inclusive, basic room tariff used to be 12 Shs and 6 Pence (less than US$1) a day. Now the cost of laundering a plain shirt at the hotel is twice that amount. Such is the price of the passing of time.

Rickshaw at Victoria Falls.

The hotel's logo, an African lion and Egyptian Sphinx, reveal that it was created as part of the mythology and dream of a bygone era, of a railway linking the Cape and Cairo with trains steaming across a map highlighted by unbroken British colonial pink.

The Victoria Falls Hotel, the oldest operating hotel in the country, has outlived and outgrown those dreams. Now, upgraded once more, it is the resort's premier historical hotel, an edifice which has adapted itself to our changing world.

The railway line from the Cape reached Victoria Falls shortly before the hotel opened. The bridge, which the hotel overlooks, was completed the following year.

The hotel opened in a simple wood and corrugated iron structure, raised to provide ventilation, minimise the damp, and keep out pests. It had 12 single and four double rooms and was managed by an Italian who was credited with introducing "ping pong" to Southern Rhodesia long before there was a Chinese Embassy. The present dining room was the whole original hotel.

The chef was a Frenchman, the barman an American from Chicago, the waiters Arabs. Foreign royals were among the first guests and the hotel was swiftly extended with two railway engine sheds.

Originally the rail tracks ran between the hotel and gorge. But torrential rain in 1908 washed away the track which was relaid just behind the hotel where it runs today.

The walk and rickshaw rides to the Falls were to prove arduous and tiring for many of the elderly hotel guests, and a rail trolley service was introduced. It was to carry two million visitors over the next 37 years. Gravitation took the trolleys downhill, "natives" pushed them back.

But by 1995 the annual figure for tourists on the Zimbabwean side of the river had leapt to an astounding 300,000. That represented a fourfold increase in less than a decade.

To cater for their needs the number of hotels increased tenfold and their sleeping capacity to 2,100 beds a night. In addition, 14 "low impact" lodges were opened, sleeping a further 250 people.

Supermarkets, restaurants, ice cream parlours, curio shops, tour operators and agents, increasingly took hold of Victoria Falls. As the scramble for the tourist dollar accelerated, even more hotels and lodges sprang up, one blocking a game migration route and raising its concrete head above the tree line.

By the nineties there was hardly a "Blimp" in sight on the streets. The more upmarket tourists left their upmarket hotels in comfortable minibuses for guided tours where they saw everything — and nothing. Backpackers, mainly visiting Victoria Falls for the whitewater rafting and bunji jumping, had increasingly taken over the streets.

"Victoria Falls today is an adventure centre," said Mike Davis of Shearwater which specialises in whitewater rafting, bunji and canoeing. "It's the river, the rapids and the dive from the bridge which bring the bulk of visitors today, not the Falls.

United Touring Company (UTC) vehicle outside Frontiers Adventures which offers the full range of adventures.

They are secondary." Sadly, he is probably right.

Strategically removed from all this is the real Victoria Falls town, Chinotimba township. The Falls town was designed and built for 8,000 people. Today it houses over three times that number and the population is growing by 14 per cent a year as a result of migration by job-seekers. That is over five times the national average.

Shearwater canoeists enjoy the evening sunset on the Zambezi River.

In Chinotimba, a sprawling shanty town has erupted, housing workers to meet the tourist demands. Many of the houses are no more than shacks, sanitation and fresh water almost non-existent.

The Zambian side of Victoria Falls remains less developed, as if caught in a time warp. Livingstone, once Zambia's capital, a few km north of the Falls, has seen better days. Developed as an administrative and trading centre with an industrial base, the town today is in decline. Out of a work force of 50,000, only 2,000 people are still employed in the industrial sector and 1,000 in tourism.

Less than half of Livingstone's registered businesses are still operating. The decline in employment, poverty, poor security, the highest AIDS rate in Zambia, and the general state of decay, are presently all factors militating against tourism development.

So is Zambia's decision to impose a US$50 single entry visa fee on British visitors, the largest non-regional national group visiting Zimbabwe, in retaliation for Britain requiring Zambians to have visas.

But there is an up-side. The population growth rate in Livingstone is only 2.6 per cent. Some repairs and maintainance, coupled with a coat of paint, could transform the run-down external facade. And, unlike Victoria Falls town, Livingstone still has land for development.

However, at the moment Zambia is casting a covetous eye at Zimbabwe, watching the number of tourists and their dollars roll into town.

Perhaps there is a lesson here to be learned from the relationship that prevailed between Kenya and Tanzania. Kenya, like Zimbabwe, with little thought for the assets they were destroying, chased tourists and their money to a point when tourists have now begun to shun Kenya.

Tanzania, like Zambia, watched enviously, in large part a victim of its own ineptitude. But in the longer term, Tanzania, not Kenya, stands to be the beneficiary. It has preserved its assets and generally controlled the numbers of visitors. If it learns from Kenya's mistakes it will become one of Africa's prime destinations. Zambia, too, needs to look at the broader lessons.

Controlled tourism to preserve assets and an area's special qualities are essential if a destination is not to lose its allure. But with Victoria Falls bringing in US$50 million a year for Zimbabwe, controls are not uppermost in most people's minds.

---

### Stark advice

A Southern Rhodesian government guide to Victoria Falls, published in the 1930s, contained the following advice for visitors to the rain forest:

"Waterproofs — Visitors are advised to provide themselves with mackintoshes and goloshes (or boots) when traversing the Rain Forest, or when exposed to the spray-clouds. Oilskins and sou'-westers can be hired from the hotel... When spray from the Falls is heavy, visitors will find it an advantage to wear a bathing costume only underneath the mackintosh".

Swimming, golf, tennis ("balls and native ball-boys are supplied"), and fishing were all listed sports. A 15-minute flight over the Falls cost £1, the hotel had a darkroom for photographers, and the clothing advice recommended sunshades for the ladies and wide-brimmed felt hats for gentlemen who might prefer a topee (pith helmet) in the hotter months.

---

Those who saw Victoria Falls 40 years and more ago in its near pristine state were lucky. Maybe then it was a contradiction, a site for the privileged few to visit. But today it is even more of a contradiction, a World Heritage Site in the grip of greed and envy.

David Martin

# GEOLOGY

Like a vast snake, the seven gorges below Victoria Falls scythe their way across the flat landscape as if escaping the restrictive embrace of the narrow, precipitous drop and cauldron immediately below.

Aerial picture showing the gorges below Victoria Falls.

That was not always how it appeared. One-hundred-and-fifty million years ago in the Jurassic Period, the supercontinent, Gondwanaland, split giving birth to today's Africa, Asia, Australia, Antarctica, New Zealand and South America.

The resulting upheaval opened vast cracks in the earth's surface and over the next 20 million or so years molten basalt lava from the earth's mantle (about 50 km beneath the surface) oozed through and into these cracks.

Basalt is a dark igneous rock ore produced by melting an earlier rock. At Victoria Falls two types of basalt are found. One is the fine-grained, dark-bluish rock seen in the gorge walls. The other, on paths from The Victoria Falls Hotel to the Falls, is purplish in colour, filled with almond-shaped white minerals often coated with green skin.

A solid basalt sheet remained after the upheaval and into this the Zambezi River, long after the lava had cooled, was to finally cut its way.

Just how thick is the lava is a matter of speculation. One expert estimated it might be as much as 300 metres, others have put it at much more. Little is known about the geology in the 100 million years after the lava cooled other than that the climate is thought to have been arid.

Certainly when the lava erupted there were lakes and deserts around, now preserved as sandy sedimentary rocks. The base of the lavas can be seen on some of the islands in Lake Kariba. Here the desert sands below have been baked to a bright orange colour by the hot lavas. Where the lavas have erupted into lakes they have formed metre-size balls or "pillars" with fine-grained chilled edges.

Other deposits formed on top of the eroded basalts. The lowest lying and oldest rock contains chalcedony, a type of quartz which forms semi-precious stones like agate and onyx. It is flint-like and was used to make stone tools by prehistoric people.

On top of the one-to-two-metre-thick, chalcedony-rich layer there is sandstone of similar thickness. Above, and now gradually receding, come the Kalahari Sand deposits which were blown into Zambia and Zimbabwe from Botswana 12 to 15 million years ago in a spasmodic sandstorm which lasted until about one million years ago.

The whole drainage system of southern/central Africa adds a further dimension to the protracted birth and present course of the Zambezi River and the very existence of Victoria Falls.

Southern Africa is like an upturned dish. The coastal belt is generally narrow, flat and low lying. Further inland this varying width of strip gives way to an escarpment, precipitous in places, long and steep in others.

Streams and rivers rise above the escarpment which is 1,000 to 1,400 metres above sea level. Some flow into lakes. Others must find their way down the escarpment to the sea.

As a result, all of the main rivers in southern/central Africa have falls or rapids as they drop towards the sea. That is an inevitable part of the levelling out process. Victoria Falls is the most spectacular point in this descent.

What is less pre-ordained is the course they follow. The types of rock they encounter dictates their course.

This second gorge from The Victoria Falls Hotel captures much of the attraction: the spray from the Falls, a rainbow, the bridge, a bunji jumper suspended and the river below.

Thus, geologists say, until the river broke through the vertical cracks (called joints), the Zambezi's upper reaches flowed into a vast inland lake and, maybe, earlier into the Limpopo River further south on the border with South Africa.

That inland lake was known as the Greater palaeo-lake Makgadikgadi, palaeo simply meaning ancient or old. Fossil remains indicate it covered about 60,000 square km (roughly the size of present-day Lake Victoria) and encompassed the Makgadikgadi Pans, the southern Okavango and Chobe Swamps, all in Botswana.

Before the birth of the Zambezi River, Greater palaeo-lake Makgadikgadi existed, as did the Middle Zambezi River which is the Lake

Kariba section below Victoria Falls and the gorges, stretching to where the river passes into the Lower Zambezi through Mozambique and on to the Indian Ocean. But the lake and Middle Zambezi were not connected and Victoria Falls did not exist.

Fossil evidence suggests that global warming leading to climatic changes was responsible for joinin Greater palaeo-lake Makgadikgadi with the Middle Zambezi and creating Victoria Falls.

The Zambian side during the dry season shows indications of Victoria Falls future course

At the time of the last inter-glacial period before the beginning of the last Ice Age, the world temperature was on average some two degrees centigrade hotter than today.

This caused localised and probably very slow flooding (not to be confused with the Biblical "Great Flood" and Noah's Ark), during which Greater palaeo-lake Makgadikgadi overflowed into the basalt basin.

Thereafter, the floodwaters gouged their way through to join the Middle Zambezi in the process creating the Zambezi River and the first Victoria Falls. Using a modern metaphor it would be like a bath overflowing with the water gradually flowing out into a gutter in the street outside. After several such overflows the bath water would cut a channel and the overflow (or river) would change course.

Lake Makgadikgadi, unable to sustain itself because evaporation exceeded inflow without the input of the Upper Zambezi, dried up and is today called Makgadikgadi Pans.

Through the basalt plate to the east, the young Zambezi River forced its way. At first, it was steep and irregular, which it still is in places such as Victoria Falls and Batoka Gorge.

As it matured, as is the case away from the Falls and rapids, it broadened, flattened out, smoothly moving towards the Indian Ocean adjoining Mozambique on the southeast African coast.

From its source near Kalene Hill in northern Zambia, the 2,700 km Zambezi River flows southwest into Angola before returning to Zambia

Water plunges over the Falls into the chasm.

flowing south through the Barotse Plain, on to the Caprivi Swamps. It is joined there by the Chobe River, and then flows east to where four countries — Botswana, Namibia, Zambia and Zimbabwe — meet. It then heads east through Kariba into Mozambique before flowing into the Indian Ocean.

The Zambezi is Africa's fourth longest river and during its varied journey it drops 1,585 feet (483 metres) before reaching the sea.

Geographers refer to Victoria Falls, and other sharp drops along a river's course, as "nick-points" which form part of the river's flattening-out process so that it meets the sea on level terms.

Livingstone wrongly speculated that the Falls resulted from a cataclysmic fracturing of the earth's crust. On the contrary, they have eroded over millions of years with the river continually probing and cutting its way through weaknesses in the Jurassic Period plate.

Very gradually the shear might and volume of the water has worn its way through the vertical cracks in the basalt, which may have been formed by shrinkage as the molten lava cooled or by later "faults", and which were filled with materials almost as soft as clay.

The cracks or fissures through which the Zambezi River charted its course run in an east-west direction. Over millions of years the focal point of Victoria Falls as we know it today has varied with one fall abandoned as the pressure of water created a new one.

Thus, those gorges further downstream were once, in retreating order, what is today known as Victoria Falls. The Second Gorge and the Boiling Pot show clearly how this evolutionary process worked.

This gorge still bears the scars, moulded by water action, of where the Falls once fell and the Boiling Pot marks the point where the lip of the Second Gorge plunged when the weight of water finally overcame it.

All of this means that today's Victoria Falls are only a temporary point of passage in the constant (albeit very gradual), process of the aging of the Zambezi River.

Already there are signs of the river changing course yet again. In human terms the process is very slow but the probability is that the next main Falls will develop on the Zimbabwean bank at Devil's Cataract while the Zambian side increasingly dries up.

# ARCHAEOLOGY

To the untutored eye, Victoria Falls and its environs may appear to contain little of note other than the Zambezi River, the spray and roar of the Falls, and the whitewater rapids below.

But behind this facade there lies much of the story of the evolution of mankind from our forebears, *Australopithecus afarensis*, through *Homo habilis, Homo erectus, Homo sapiens*, and finally on to contemporary *Homo sapiens sapiens*.

*Australopithecus afarensis* (Southern ape) is the earliest known ancestor of modern humans. They lived in southern and eastern Africa five million years ago and were small in stature, mainly vegetarians and bipedal, meaning they could walk on their hind feet.

The end of the period known as the Pliocene, 2.5 million years ago, was the period of *Homo habilis* who fashioned crude tools. This was the earliest cultural stage of humans in which simple stone tools were developed for chopping, pounding, cutting and scraping.

The next major development was the emergence of *Homo erectus* who had increased brain capacity, and produced more refined tools such as hand-axes and cleavers.

An early Stone Age tool found in the Zambezi basin.

*Homo sapiens sapiens* or modern people began to emerge about 100,000 years ago, manufacturing ever more sophisticated tools and weapons.

Development through these biological and cultural phases was agonisingly slow, quickening with the onset of village farming over the last six thousand to seven thousand years.

At Victoria Falls the visitor will frequently see water-rounded and polished stones, mainly chalcedony and agates referred to in the geological section. These are particularly common in the gravel at the Falls, especially near the Eastern Cataract on the Zambian side, and on the road to the Fifth Gorge.

According to the anthropologist J. Desmond Clark. "…a very large percentage of the glazed and patinated stones are flakes, cores and retouched tools made by prehistoric man."

The cultural contents of the gravels were first recognised at the beginning of this century. Studies since then, largely through comparisons with other areas (notably east Africa), have established a chronological framework of the past several million years.

The gravels containing the flakes, cores and retouched stones feature prominently on the ridges that mark the zigzag course of the Zambezi River through the gorges downstream from the Falls.

They are to be found most easily on the Zambian side of the river, five to seven km west of Livingstone on the Nakatindi Road, and on the Livingstone-Victoria Falls road south of Maramba River.

The stone implements and animal fossil remains are of differing ages and reveal periods of fluctuating river activity and settlement, as well as temperature and rainfall variations.

Justifiably, the lay person may wonder how much of the past can really be read from this seeming jumble of rock fragments, bones and sediments.

"When all these different kinds of sediments are arranged in a sequence from oldest to youngest and the stone implements and fossils they contain are compared, a developing pattern of increasing technology and typological complexity is clearly seen," says Clark.

Geologists and palaeo-ecologists can ascertain past temperatures and humidity, palaeontology, faunal zones and the occurrences of extinct mammals, plants and fish.

What remains at Victoria Falls is less than in the Rift Valley of east Africa where conditions are more conducive to preservation. But the perishable remains (wooden and bone instruments, food-waste and traces of dwellings) found in east Africa taken together with the imperishable remains (stone implements) found in the Zambezi valley help piece together the prehistoric jigsaw.

In the Victoria Falls area there is evidence of human presence as far back as the Oldowan Industry, named after Olduvai Gorge (a Maasai word for wild sisal, spelt *Oldupai* in Maasai) in Tanzania, which occurred around two million years ago.

Olduvai Gorge, referred to as the birthplace of humans

In the highest and earliest gravels, intentionally cut and heavily worn choppers flaked from chalcedony are found. These were used by early people for chopping and cutting, thereby indicating skills as tool makers, prowess in butchering animals, probable use of skins, as well as cultural and intellectual levels.

From the sites where they are found, further evidence emerges regarding ecological and geographical behaviour, where prehistoric people were resident or transient, and to what degree their periods of residence were affected by the level of the river, temperature and rainfall.

In addition to the choppers, small stone flakes used between the thumb and finger for more precise work, and stones with at least six faces used for hammering and bashing, have also been found.

It is these sorts of finds that justify the cross-referencing with the more complete Olduvai finds. *Australopithecines* at Olduvai only used natural objects as tools; *Homo habilis* – the earliest toolmaker or, more scientifically, the first person with the ability to make tools – is believed to have lived at both sites.

Those early hominids, scientists deduce, lived in small groups operating from a home-base where the young, who were parent-dependent about as long as children are today, were raised and taught skills.

They hunted small game, sometimes larger animals, and scavenged meat from recently dead animals.

Also found in the same high-level gravels at Victoria Falls are large, pear-shaped handaxes associated with the earliest stages of the Acheulian Industrial Complex which occurred around one million years ago, coinciding with the transition from the early to developed Oldowan Industry. These tools demonstrate the beginnings of what we now refer to as "standardisation".

Charles Darwin and T.H. Huxley both speculated that the toolmaker, or *Homo habilis,* originated in the tropics, possibly Africa, and between one and one-and-a-half million years ago spread fairly rapidly into Europe and Asia.

In the Zambezi Valley, late Acheulian people produced increasingly refined hand-axes and cleavers, possibly for butchering large animals, from quartz, quartzite, or lava.

An elephant crossing the Zambiezi River above Victoria Falls. Once they were hunted by early humans and later almost exterminated by the first white hunters and settlers.

The next cultural artefacts, appearing in the sandscarp on Mbwile Drive west of Livingstone and the railway cuttings just south of Victoria Falls town, are from what is known as the Sangoan Industrial Complex which occurred about 100,000 years ago.

The sites where these artefacts have been found are the earliest totally undisturbed ones in the Victoria Falls area. The sites afforded excellent vantage points over the valley, were close to the raw materials used to fashion tools, and contain what are believed to be woodworking tools.

While the Acheulian hand-axe is still found, it is now of less significance. The new hand-axes are generally smaller and more pointed; picks or core axes, similar to those used by Australian aboriginals, appear for the first time.

Throughout this evolutionary process from *Homo habilis* to *Homo erectus* and finally *Homo sapiens sapiens*, one sees evidence of the increased sophistication and the reduction in weight of the early basic tool kit.

From the Middle Stone Age around 100,000 to 20,000 years ago, evidence of the development of new tools emerges. One of these is the spear, regarded as a major invention of the Stone Age, which was later tipped with poison from the pod of the *Swartzia* tree.

Another important weapon is a sphere-like stone thought to have been used like the South American *bolas,* being hurled in a thong at a small animal entangling its legs.

The evidence also shows that the Victoria Falls area was considered a particularly favourable area by hunter-gatherer people, although their periods of residence and density varied.

Fish provided an important protein diet-supplement; oil-rich *mungongo* nuts pounded into a porridge were the principal vegetable staple, and the fruits of baobab, *marula,* wild figs, dates, the Barotse plums and African oranges were also eaten.

The discovery of beads shows that a degree of personal adornment was practised, and red ochre and a ferric oxide stone called haematite were used by people to paint themselves, much as the East African Masai *moran* still do.

The exact date of the appearance of modern people *(Homo sapiens sapiens)* in the Zambezi Valley is in some doubt. Most likely it was around the last part of the Acheulian, putting it about 100,000 years ago. Certainly, it was a very long time before the arrival of Dr Livingstone!

A short distance upstream from the Falls is the "Big Tree", (pictured left), a baobab where the early white settlers are said to have camped and from where they crossed the river from the Old Drift to Livingstone before the bridge was built.

By baobab standards it is neither a particularly big nor old tree. It is some 20 metres tall and 16 metres around its trunk. And it is only about 1,000 years old, a third of the way to its life expectation.

Generally found in Africa's more arid areas, the baobab is steeped in mythology. Legend has it that the branches hold up the sky. Drink an infusion of the bark and you become mighty and strong; drink water the seeds have been soaked in and you are protected against crocodiles. Another baobab legend holds that God was so angry with man's behaviour that he deliberately planted the tree upsidedown.

The bark is woody and fibrous, the trunk stores a prodigous amount of water rather like a camels hump, the seeds are high in vitamin C, and the acidic pulp from the dried pods forms the powder from which cream of tartar is made.

Livingstone was furious at a French botanist, Michael Adanson (the botanical name of the tree is *Adansonia digitata*), who dated one tree as being 5,150 years old. That was before the creation, and in Livingstone's view nothing could predate that. But then the doctor was also wrong about how Victoria Falls was created.

# CLIMATE

Over millions of years Victoria Falls has been subjected to consequential temperature swings. Once the Zambezi Valley was filled by glaciers; the Falls themselves and the connecting of the Upper and Middle Zambezi River systems occurred because of global warming.

Today the climate is classified as sub-tropical hot and arid, and the swings in temperature and related climatic activity are – in the short-term – less extreme and more predictable. Nevertheless, there are still marked climatic variations during four seasons as follows:

**Hot season**
**Main rainy season**
**Post rainy season**
**Cool dry season**

The prelude to the rains in September heralds the hottest months of the year. Clouds gather in blue skies and daytime temperatures can soar into

The dark spray from Victoria Falls hangs eerily in the sky above the rising sun and concrete lampposts on the main street.

the upper 30s C, sometimes well beyond. Its a fine time for whitewater rafters, but oppressively hot outdoors.

The rains, which usually arrive in October/November, and end in March/April, bring welcome relief. It usually rains in the afternoon and evening. In November/December the water flow over the Falls is at its lowest level, which can make viewing disappointing.

But birdwatching, with the arrival of migrants, is particularly good in this period, electric storms can be spectacular, and the multi-coloured, pearl-shaped, raindrop orbs clinging to lush green vegetation in brilliant sunshine, invite memorable photographs.

From February through to around June, as the waters from the vast northern catchment area arrive, the Falls are at their peak. The clouds of spray rise ever higher and can be seen 30 km away. Beyond the rain forest a drenching is guaranteed.

A visitor rents an umbrella from a vendor.

June to September are the most popular months with visitors. Daytime temperatures are around 17-27 degrees C dropping by at least a third at night. In what locals call the winter months (June/July) they can drop to 4-8 degrees C. You are advised to bring warm clothes.

Despite these seeming extremes Zimbabwe justifiably claims to have one of the world's most idyllic climates. That in part accounts for why you find so many climatic refugees in Zimbabwe as well as visitors from the rigours of the northern and southern hemispheres.

# HISTORY

The Khoisan, locally known as Kwengo and derogatorily referred to as Bushmen, are the first known residents in the Victoria Falls area. Their numbers were relatively few and they were hunter-gatherers.

These Late Stone Age people achieved an effective degree of socio-economic integration stretching back several thousand years. Initially, their life-styles were not greatly affected by the arrival of Early Iron Age residents in the area around 2,000 years ago.

However, as competition for land increased, the Khoisan were gradually pushed out of the area, moving to today's northern Namibia and Botswana where small numbers still exist.

The hunter-gatherers lived a semi-nomadic family life, whereas the Iron Age farming economy demanded semi-permanent villages, intensive land use, and forest clearance, all of which restricted grazing for wildlife in an area with an already marginal carrying capacity.

The comparatively large village populations of the Early Iron Age people, and their closer affinity to land and territory, were further obstacles to cohabitation. As a result, by the middle of the first millennium A.D. the Khoisan appear to have totally vacated the area, leaving it to Early Iron Age agricultural village communities.

Khoisan woman and child.

The earliest Iron Age villages were small, semi-permanent, scattered, and only occupied for brief periods. In this, they did not differ too much from the Khoisan. But within a short period the villages took on a more permanent nature, and were occupied by communities numbering up to 200 who lived in them for 20 or more years.

The Early Iron Age inhabitants produced pottery, smelted iron ore, manufactured artefacts from iron and copper, and are thought to have traded in ivory. Huts were thatched with grass. Overall the economy was basically a simple subsistence one.

The ridged thatching of an Ndebele hut.

The sites they chose for their villages were normally situated on the edge of seasonally waterlogged, flat-bottomed valleys (*dambos*) to graze their cattle, goats and sheep, plant gardens near the water-edge, and draw water from wells they dug.

Copper, as ornaments and ingots, have been fund at several sites in the Victoria Falls area. As copper is not known to have been mined in the area, this implies the existence of a local and long-distance trading network.

The items traded locally included pottery and salt, while beads and cowrie shells indicate long-distance trading with the coast.

Cultural advancement progressed into what is known as the Kalomo Tradition. Because this was an evolutionary process there are no neat start and cut-off dates. Rather what one sees is a gradual change in lifestyle.

Villages became fewer, with a smaller number of occupants, probably less than 50 in a community. The economy of those associated with the Kalomo Tradition was very similar to the earlier, larger villages, with agriculture and animal husbandry accounting for about half the community's activity, and hunting and gathering accounting for the rest.

So what one finds is a society in transition from the old hunter- gatherer Khoisan communities to the subsistence communities that followed.

During this transition some smelting was done and light wood-working tools and arrowheads were produced. Blunt, thick needles found at excavated sites suggest hides were sewn, while copper finds show that trading patterns continued.

One important craft in these Kalomo Tradition villages was the manufacture of decorated, clay pottery receptacles. From these vessels, archaeologists have dated the Kalomo occupation of the Batoka plateau and Zambezi Valley as the beginning of the 10th century.

Next came what is known as the Early Tonga Tradition. Archaeological evidence dates this as occurring by the early 12th century when villages in the area began to absorb the Tonga-speaking peoples who moved into the area from southern Zambia.

A beer pot.

The Kalomo and Tonga integrated in existing Kalomo villages. This cohabitation brought with it important cultural changes with a greater number of soils being exploited for agricultural purposes (see *Kariba: Nyaminyami's Kingdom,* in this series).

For the first time, clay figurines, most commonly depicting human or animal figures, appear. Iron hoe-blades become more frequent indicat-

33

ing an increase in smithying, farming, or both. The number of cattle bones indicate that more domestic stock was kept.

Exactly who the earliest proto-Tongas were, where they came from, and their reasons for moving to the area, are confused by differing and contradictory oral histories.

But the first proto-Tonga occupants of the area appear to have been the Leya who migrated from Zambia's Southern Province and/or Central Province. They mainly lived on the north bank of the Zambezi River with smaller numbers living on the south bank. They probably arrived in the area in the 12th century in search of permanent water.

One account says that the founder of the Rozvi kingdom sent a chief named Ne-Mhanwe north on an expedition against the Shangwe living near the Zambezi River in the Sebungwe district. He conquered the Shangwe and settled in the area.

One further proto-Tonga group, the Toka, must be mentioned here. This is probably the largest of the groups occupying the north bank of the Zambezi River in the Victoria Falls area. Culturally and linguistically the Toka are very similar to the Leya, separated only by the historical roots of their rulers.

Localised and regional skirmishes ebbed and flowed through the area in successive waves with Leya fighting each other over land. The Lozi, led by King Ngombala (the Enslaver of Nations), defeated part of the Leya group.

Next the Kololo leader, Sebitwane, fleeing the *Mfecane* further south, invaded the region with his Sotho army and defeated the Lozi. Finally, in 1864, the Lozi regained their territory defeating the Kololo.

The languages, customs and beliefs of different groups in the Victoria Falls area are very similar. Toka and Leya, for instance, which are both Tonga dialects and Bantu languages, are mutually intelligible.

The Leya, like the Tonga, are a matrilineal people with a high priestess *(Bedyango* or *Ina-Sing'andu)*, selected from among the chief's aunts and sisters, having a highly ritualistic influence over the land. Her rituals used to include preventing disasters during wars, droughts and epidemics.

She officiated at births, marriages and deaths and was the final arbitrator in the choice of a new chief. However, missionary influences and

Today donkey carts provide one of the most common forms of rural transport.

contemporary political circumstances, have reduced the importance of this office.

Another Tonga-related group in the area, the Subiya, are respected and feared as great magicians. One Subiya leader is credited with releasing an epidemic in the area, another with releasing mist which blinded enemies ensuring he was never defeated in battle.

The royal drums of one group of Leya are credited with miraculous powers independently sounding the danger signal and the battle call. One drum *(makuwakuwa)* is credited with escaping capture by leaping into the Zambezi River where it sounded for many years thereafter.

The Victoria Falls was a place of worship to the ancestors for at least three local groups. One missionary wrote that local inhabitants "believe it is haunted by a malevolent and cruel divinity".

Graves were surrounded by elephant tusks as a show of reverence, as was the case with the Middle Zambezi Tonga. This custom has also gone, a victim of ivory hunters and traders initially, and more recently of hunting controls.

Other traditions, particularly away from the urban centres, are retained. Intermediaries still sing the praises of prospective husbands and negotiate a bride price. Food staples such as maize remain.

Upper, central incisor teeth are still pulled out as a mark of ethnic identity and fashion. Elderly women still wear the Victorian-influenced *musisi,* a loose blouse over layers of skirts, and some old men still wear the Lozi kilt, the *siziba.*

A maize granery

Among the Leya, songs remain the highest form of literary expression. They are also skilled in utilitarian pottery (bowls, water pots and so on), but not sculpture. Their ornate and intricate beadwork is notable as is the Subiya patterned pottery.

## COLONIAL

The late Zambian historian and Director of the Livingstone Museum, Kafungulwa Mubitana, once noted that Livingstone's eloquent reports about Victoria Falls brought "... many adventurers from Europe and the Cape, from whose writings much historical and ethnographical information may be gathered about the peoples of the Victoria Falls region as seen by outsiders."

But most of these writings, Mubitana observed, were superficial. People were regarded as distractions and the writings were frequently derogatory about Africans.

In the 15th century, Portuguese navigators, including Vasco da Gama, rounded the Cape of Good Hope for the first time, establishing forts at

Kilwa and Sofala in 1505 and Mozambique Island in 1558. Inland expeditions followed from the Mozambique coast, but they are thought to have penetrated the area only as far as the Middle Zambezi.

Generally, maps of the African interior were figments of the map-makers' imaginations. This ignorance — and previous falsification — was acknowedged by 19th century map-makers who, instead of resorting to a mix of fact and fiction, wisely chose to leave much of the interior blank.

The first impact on the Victoria Falls area from European settlement in general came about in an indirect way early in the 19th century. The Kololo's northern migration, leading to the conquest of the Lozi, resulted from drought and land pressure in South Africa following the rapid increase in European settlement there.

**Agents of Imperialism**
European explorers, hunters, traders and missionaries followed soon after the Kololo migration, and on 16 November 1855 Livingstone saw for the first time *Mosi-oa-Tunya,* which he renamed Victoria Falls. The Falls had in fact been known as *Mosi-va-tuna* "the smoke that sounds", by Europeans since 1840.

On 3 August 1851, William Cotton Oswell, an English hunter who supported Livingstone on a journey from the Cape, marked on a manuscript map in reference to Victoria Falls, "Waterfall, spray seen 10 miles off". The map was not produced until 1900 and, apparently, Livingstone and Oswell had not attempted to get closer.

Curiously, and inexplicably, a map published in London in 1852 by William Desborough Cooley in his book *Inner Africa Laid Open,* accurately pinpoints the Falls three years before Livingstone's "discovery".

A Portuguese trader, Silva Antonio Francisco Porto, and a Hungarian, Ladislaus Magyar, may also have reached the Falls before Livingstone. Subsequently, when asked to justify his claim that he was the first European to see the Falls when Silva Porto might have preceded him, Livingstone is said to have retorted that he did not consider a "half-caste" (Portuguese) to be a European!

Livingstone had visited the Falls wearing two hats, the first as an explorer, the second as a representative of the London Missionary Society who subsequently withdrew their support, saying Livingstone was primarily an explorer.

However, on his next mission to Africa, Livingstone travelled as "H.M. Consul for the East Coast of Africa to the south of Zanzibar and for the unexplored interior". The first rumblings of the European Scramble for Africa had begun and Britain needed more information to stake its claims.

Livingstone's mission for the British goverment was "to survey and report on the country watered by the lower Zambezi". He began his journey from Quelimane in Mozambique, travelled through Malawi's Shire Highlands, and made his second and last visit to the Victoria Falls area.

The significance of this journey must be understood in conjunction with subsequent colonial history. Britain not only perceived Mozambique as Portuguese territory, but also as the access point to the interior. So the British established an enclave, Chinde, near the mouth of the Zambezi to ensure their access.

Insofar as the interior was concerned, Britain became the coloniser of the whole centre of Africa including Malawi, Northern and Southern Rhodesia. This prevented the Portuguese, whose colonising power was in decline, from laying claim to the swathe of land from the Atlantic to the Indian Ocean which Silva Porto had explored.

Having thwarted Portugal's east-west thrust, Britain sought to further her own north-south ambitions by laying claim to an unbroken stretch of land connecting the Cape to Cairo. This would pass through South Africa, and the territories that were later to become Southern and Northern Rhodesia, Tanganyika (German East Africa), Kenya and Uganda, and finally Sudan and Eygpt.

While the British now directed Livingstone's journeys to fit their plans for the future East Africa, other explorers, hunters, traders and missionaries made their way to the Victoria Falls area.

Notable among these were James Chapman and Thomas Baines. Chapman and Baines reached the Falls from Walvis Bay in Namibia thereby opening another potential colonial link. Baines, who had been sacked by Livingstone, died a pauper, but left a legacy of fine paintings of the area.

Thomas Baines.

Buffalo hunt in the rain forest, Thomas Baines, 1863.

By 1870, at least 25 Europeans had visited the Falls.  In 1874/75 the numbers doubled and now the time had come to establish a more permanent presence in the area.

This new thrust was spearheaded by George Westbeech, an English trader, and his hunter partner, George "Elephant" Phillips.  They opened a trading post at Pandamatenga on the "hunters' road" from Shoshong to Kazungula in 1871.  They became in effect the first European tourist agents in the area acting for safari pioneers. One of these was Harry Ware who, as early as 1876, advertised hunting expeditions and sight-seeing in and around Victoria Falls in the London sporting magazine, *The Field.*

Two other "tourist agents", Juma and Susi, must be mentioned here for they preceded Ware into the area by 21 years.  They came from the Tanzanian Indian Ocean port of Bagamoyo, north of Dar es Salaam (Haven of Peace in Arabic), which is opposite Zanzibar.  Research has shown that it was they who guided Livingstone into the area where the local Kololo showed him Victoria Falls.

Another aspect of the creation of that permanent presence was the opening of Christian mission stations.  The London Missionary Society, at Livingstone's suggestion, had tried to do so in 1860.  But disease drove surviving missionaries out of the area.

In 1878, this time through the Paris Evangelical Society, Francois Coillard and his wife reached Leshoma, one of Westbeech's trading stations at Kazungula, today on the Botswana/Zimbabwe border 20 km south of the Zambezi.

Coillard was admirably prepared for his mission. He was transferred from Basutoland (now Lesotho), where he had learned the Sotho dialect introduced by the Kololo to the northern part of the Victoria Falls area which the Kololo had conquered 30 years earlier. At Leshoma the Coillards were visited by Major A. de Serpa Pinto, a Portuguese explorer on a trans-Africa mission in the footsteps of Silva Porto. British and Portuguese competition for the African interior was still alive at this point.

Francois Coillard.

The colonial powers met in Berlin in 1883/84. Britain, under pressure from merchants and investors, blocked Portugal's expansionist plans, taking central Africa for itself. The French took many colonies in West and North Africa, the Germans took today's Tanzania, Namibia, Rwanda and Burundi, the Belgians the Congo, and the Portuguese managed to retain Angola, Mozambique and Cape Verde. This was the culmination of "The Scramble for Africa".

Britain was reluctant to embark on further imperial expansion because of the cost. But men like Cecil Rhodes, who had recently obtained control of South Africa's Kimberley diamond fields and the recently discovered Witwatersrand gold, believed further riches lay to the north. He needed the cover of the British government to further his own ambitions.

### Agents of influence
Westbeech, Coillard and other traders and missionaries, who had established close ties with local African rulers, were to become what some years later British intelligence would refer to as "agents of influence".

They were not agents in the strict contemporary usage of the word. Rather they were locally influential having established a degree of rapport with local African rulers. They were, in reality, the "eyes and ears" of imperialism well-placed to further British interests.

Using the network of traders and missionaries, Rhodes and others acquired concessions from local rulers such as Lobengula, King of the

Ndebele. This in turn led to the creation in 1889 of Rhodes' British South African Company (BSAC), the granting of a Royal Charter by Britain, and subsequent "Pioneer Column" invasion.

Westbeech had died in 1888 and Ware, on the basis of his previous association with Westbeech, persuaded the Lozi leader, King Lewanika, to sign a mineral concession in 1889. Rhodes later bought the concession persuading Lewanika his treaty was with the British government and not the commercial BSAC.

It is possible that the local African leaders felt, or were encouraged to feel, threatened by Boer expansion from the south and by continuing Portuguese colonial ambitions. But in seeking "British protection" they were courting new risks, not simply with the British Queen but with Rhodes, the real driving force.

British indifference towards local rulers such as Lewanika emerges as early as 1890 in a draft treaty creating boundaries between British and Portuguese colonies. In this, Lewanika's domain was to be bisected; he was not consulted about this proposal.

The treaty was later amended as a result of the concession Frank Lochner, a BSAC agent, had concluded with Lewanika. And, also in 1890, Germany was granted the expansion of German South West Africa (now Namibia) to include the Caprivi Strip and access to the Zambezi and the Falls.

In 1900 at Victoria Falls, because the dubious Lochner treaty did not formally cede administration of the area to the BSAC and was also doubtful in terms of the BSAC Royal Charter, a further concession agreement was signed. By now Lewanika's hands were tied and the new agreement, generally, was even less advantageous to the Lozi than the previous one.

These are the boundaries which remain in place around Victoria Falls today. By 1905, only half a century after Livingstone's first visit, the area's African rulers had had their land taken from them and the busy colonial village, to become the town of Victoria Falls, was taking root.

One of the first settlers to arrive in the area towards the end of the last century was F.J. "Mopane" Clarke. He was by all accounts a colourful character in the wild, frontier settler mould of the day.

In 1898, he built a general store, hotel and bar nine km up from the Falls at a crude settlement which was known as the Old Drift. The bar had a roulette wheel and croupier and would stay open all night if there was sufficient demand. A regular coach route from Bulawayo, which took 12 days to reach Victoria Falls, ensured a constant flow of hunters, prospectors, miners and traders.

In 1903, the European population of the settlement was recorded as being 68, with Mopane as its chief citizen. A Mr P.M. Clark, (no relation), had started river cruises by launch and canoe, and had opened a photographic studio in a mud hut.

It was the heyday of the Old Drift where hard drinking and gambling men gathered. The Zambezi Boat Club held its first regatta in 1905 and in 1910 hosted the world sculling championshp with a prize of £1,000 which, according to *The Victoria Falls Advertiser* newspaper of 3 October 1910, was won by a Mr Arnst.

P.M. Clark poses outside his photographic studio.

But the days of the Old Drift were numbered. Blackwater fever, a virulent form of malaria, was exacting a terrible toll as evidenced by the headstones in the cemetary on Riverside Drive. The only doctor and two pharmacists had died from the disease.

However, it was to be the railway line from Bulawayo and the bridge across the Zambezi River in the spray of Victoria Falls, and not malaria, which finally forced the move from the Old Drift. The new site was on Constitution Hill, and the new town was called Livingstone.

Rhodes, who never visited Victoria Falls, had expressed the wish that the bridge across the Zambezi be built so that the spray fell on the train carriages crossing it. Despite engineering advice that it should be built further upstream, building went ahead creating, in the words of the authors of the coffee-table book, *African Thunder: The Victoria Falls*, "a most hideous monument to Victorian vanity".

An early 1905 picture of the bridge nearing completion.

The motive for building the bridge at Victoria Falls in fact had nothing to do with such romantic notions as the spray falling on the carriages.

Rhodes was determined to drive a railway across the whole continent from the Cape to Cairo. His most obvious, cheapest and shortest route was to ford the Zambezi at Chirundu to the north of the easternend of today's Lake Kariba. But in 1893 large deposits of coal had been found at Wange (now wrongly spelt Hwange) and the railway was diverted through the Falls to exploit the coal.

Sir Douglas Fox designed the cantilever bridge which was built by the English firm, the Cleveland Bridge Company. It is 198 metres long, has a 152-metre central span, and is set 125 metres above the low water mark.

Construction was exacting. First a piece of string was fired across the gorge by rocket. Gradually the strength of this link was increased with thicker ropes and, finally, a three-inch-thick steel cable.

A "blondin" four-ton, electric rope-walker was attached to the cable, a bosun's chair employed to avoid the 12 km walk (which some still preferred to take), and a safety net hung 90 metres above the water.

On 31 March 1905, the two ends of the bridge, which had been built simultaneously from opposite banks, were ready to be connected. Despite all the careful calculations, they were six inches too long. Heat had expanded them. But a cool wind and the spray contracted them overnight, with the two sections fitting perfectly early the following morning.

The southern (now Zimbabwean) bank of Victoria Falls remained a scenic backwater until 1963 when the Federation of Rhodesia and

Nyasaland was wound up after a decade-long unequal partnership between settler-ruled Southern Rhodesia (Zimbabwe), Northern Rhodesia (Zambia) and Nyasaland (Malawi). Malawi and Zambia achieved majority rule immediately after Federation.

The 1965 Unilateral Declaration of Independence (UDI) from Britain by the settler leader, Ian Smith, intended to block majority rule, ensured that the potential of the Southern Rhodesian bank of Victoria Falls remained unrealised. The Zambezi River, said the late Swedish Prime Minister, Olaf Palme, as he gazed across it from the Zambian bank during the liberation war, represented "the boundary of human decency".

A mine field, part of which has not been fully removed, was sewn on either side of Victoria Falls town up to the river bank and to the main Bulawayo road to protect the town from guerrilla incursions. But this did not protect the original Elephant Hills Hotel from a missile strike which destroyed it in November 1977.

By then Smith had closed the border with Zambia for harbouring "terrorists". He recanted immediately, but Zambia kept the border closed and border guards eyed each other uneasily across the closed bridge.

On 25 August 1975, the bridge was to provide the stage for a farcical comedy. The most inappropriately named "White Train" from racially

A steam locomotive crossing the Victoria Falls bridge.

segregated South Africa parked on the bridge, its conference room exactly straddling the white line dividing Zambia and Southern Rhodesia. The meeting, which swiftly became acrimonious, was intended to break the Southern Rhodesian political impasse.

The Zambian and South African leaders told jokes and tried to put on a brave face. The Southern Rhodesian black nationalists were divided and Smith remained obdurate, refusing to bow out to majority rule.

A little over five years later, no longer able to militarily and economically sustain the war against now more cohesive black nationalists, Smith was forced to surrender. At least 30,000 people had been killed in the intervening five years, including many Zimbabweans in refugee and guerrilla camps in neighbouring countries.

With Livingstone in decline, Victoria Falls boomed in the 1990s with tourists and hotels increasing dramatically. The sleeping giant had finally stirred, bringing a whole new set of concerns.

# A WALK AROUND THE FALLS

The usual, and mildly energetic, way of touring Victoria Falls is on foot from The Victoria Falls Hotel, the town's most distinctive and historic landmark, or from the nearby car park.

Facing out from the hotel's terrace you see ahead of you the second gorge and the Victoria Falls bridge.

From the terrace follow the path leading 45 degrees to the left, past the hotel's north wing, downhill through thin, mixed woodland and into mopane woodland as the soil changes from Kalahari Sand to basalt.

The walk to the old river bed will not take you much more than 15 minutes and it is worth pausing to view the variety of grasses and birds. You are likely to see stubby-beaked Blue Waxbills, Brown and Redbilled Firefinchs with their distinctive red heads and underparts, heavily-billed Threestreaked and Crowned Tchagras with their chestnut-coloured wings.

You may also encounter a troop of baboons and Vervet monkeys. Older male baboons will

A vervet monkey stands to get a better view.

assiduously avoid direct eyecontact with you. Such eyeballing makes them feel threatened, undermining their authority over the troop when they back off. Do not feed the baboons, or any other animals you may encounter. They will become pests if you do.

For those who keep still and quiet the reward may be one of the several species of antelope who inhabit the area. The small, dull brown lizards you are most likely to see are Striped Skink. And you may see a ball of dung being propelled surprisingly rapidly across your path by a Dung Beetle using its hind legs (elephant dung is preferred).

Butterflies abound, particularly in the wetter months. During your walk you may see large, robust and fast-flying Swallowtails and Swordtails, brilliantly coloured Blues, Coppers and Hairtails known as "flying jewels", Monarchs, Milkweeds and Charaxes.

A baby strapped on a man's back and a basket balanced on a women's head show two differing cultures.

At the end of the first stage of your leisurely stroll you cross the main railway line arriving at the car park. Across the road is the entrance to Victoria Falls National Park where an entry fee is charged. The entry fee for foreigners is Z$100 and, quite bizarrely, they may give you 50 Z$2 receipts.

Once through the thatched entry gate there is an education centre with information about the area, photographs and maps. It is worth acquainting yourelf with this and you should note that the park is open from 0600 to 1800 hours daily.

A few yards away the path divides. I suggest you take the left hand path leading you to Livingstone's statue overlooking the Devil's Cataract at Viewpoint No 1.

The first Devil's Cararact view can be particularly photogenic in the late afternoon as the sun dips towards the horizon and a rainbow forms over the chasm. Across the Falls, beyond Devil's Cataract, is Cataract Island,

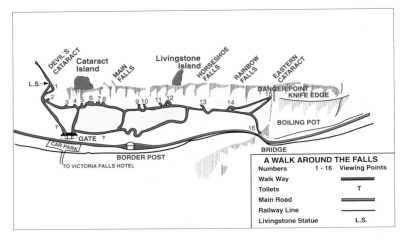

the Main Falls, Livingstone Island, Horseshoe Falls, Rainbow Falls, and finally the Eastern Cataract on the Zambian side of the Zambezi. As you move east along the pathway you will get better views of each of these.

If you have the time, and it is well worth making it, after reaching the Livingstone statue, you can walk a short distance upstream along the river bank to the park gate watching the river gather pace before hurling itself over the Falls into the narrow, whitewater gorge below. There is an abundance of water birds and you can see the damage caused by foraging elephants.

A Yellowbilled Egret above the Falls.

Moving downstream from the statue, you will pass a flight of steps on your left known as the Chain Walk. After the Chain Walk take the sign-posted, left-hand fork in the path towards the Main Falls and other 15 Viewpoints.

Once you take the fork the foliage becomes denser, more verdant, and vine-draped. You have entered the rain forest. Here the multi-storied growth is stimulated by the moisture fall-out from the Falls.

The Zambezi River behind the Devils Cataract.

From Viewpoint 2 you look directly across the gorge at Devil's Cataract. Here, and at the next two Viewing Points, you can get an idea of the river's unrelenting search for a new escape. The Devil's Cataract is several metres lower than the rest of the Falls and it is here the volume of water is concentrated year round. But there is a cleft in Cataract Island and, just maybe the river will one day gouge its new course there.

From Viewpoint 3 onwards look out for swarms of dragon-flies and for animal spoor in the mud beside the path. This Viewpoint and those up to No. 12 face Cataract Island, the Main Falls, and Livingstone Island.

From February to May, the views on this stretch, and at Danger Point facing Rainbow Falls, can be obscured by swirling spray while in November/December the water flows and those of the Eastern Cataract, tend to dry up, making viewing disappointing as well.

Viewpoint 7 will give you the best view of the Main Falls and from the right-hand corner of the viewing area you can see the Zambezi River at the bottom of the gorge below. This area is also where you will most easily see mahogany and ebony trees as well as wild orchids with their pink and purple flowers during the rainy season.

Be particularly careful at Danger Point. The rocks are very slippery when wet and you are strongly advised at all times to stick to the paths designed to ensure your safety and prevent you plunging into the gorge below.

At various places along the river-bank walk you have the option to shorten your walk. Between Viewpoints 4 and 5 there is a pathway leading straight back to the entrance. There is another between Viewpoints 12 and 13 which meanders through the southern part of the rain forest.

Tourist looks through the spray at the Main Falls.

Should you go right on to Danger Point, where the trees give way to more open spray-drenched country, you will first cross a small, rustic, timber bridge. Thereafter the trees become more widely spaced and wild, yellow gladioli grow in the rainy season.

From Viewpoint 9 you are likely to see little other than swirling clouds of spray when the river is in flood. The vegetation, continually battered by the spray, thins with only grasses and low scrubs taking root.

It is worth pausing at Viewpoint 11. Just off the path there is an all-year-round pool. Look carefully at the bottom and you may see purple freshwater crabs. Lurking nearby, waiting for unwary crabs who venture out, may be Trumpeter Hornbills who are not adverse to supplementing their fruit diet.

The Main Falls in flood.

The next left-hand branch in the pathway leads to Viewpoint 13. This is opposite Horseshoe Falls, so named because the river is carving a horseshoe shaped fissure into Livingstone Island.

Viewpoint 14 overlooks the highest of the falls, Rainbow, which is 108 metres in height. The rocks along this section to Danger Point are very slippery and great care should be exercised.

However, to obtain the best views at Danger Point (Viewpoint 15), it is necessary to climb carefully onto the rocks. Below, the two branches of the river come into view, one set of whitewater rushing from the Devil's Cataract, Main and Rainbow Falls, the other from Danger Point and the Eastern Cataract. Below you they meet in a swirling whirlpool aptly known as the Boiling Pot.

There is one last small diversion as you wind your way back to the entrance. Off to your left is Viewpoint 16 from where you can get the closest pictures of the Victoria Falls bridge.

The whole walk, even for those not enthusiastic about physical exercise, is a most enjoyable experience during which you will have seen Victoria Falls from many angles as well as some of the mammals, birds, reptiles, trees and grasses within this World Heritage Site.

# THE FUTURE

A sombre warning is contained in the *Strategic Environmental Assessment of Developments Around Victoria Falls*, a report conducted for the governments of Zambia and Zimbabwe by IUCN — The World Conservation Union.

"The Rain Forest is showing indications of stress in terms of trampled vegetation and soil erosion, the litter, especially on the Zambian side, the threat of fires during the dry season, and the visual impact of increasing numbers of visitors."

Because the two governments participated in the study, the report is somewhat veiled and it is necessary to read between the lines to understand the gravity of the situation quite rapidly unfolding at Victoria Falls.

While Livingstone's infrastructure is able

Cartoon in the Zimbabwean national newspaper, *The Herald*, skirts the point that it is up to the government to regulate the numbers of visitors and facilities.

Baboons pick through the Chinotimba rubbish dump with Lesser Egrets perched in the trees behind waiting their turn.

to absorb additional hotels, Victoria Falls has almost reached its carrying capacity.

The acceptable noise-pollution level has been exceeded; cruise boats and their jetties are disturbing wildlife and destroyed riparian vegetation; whitewater rafters are damaging traditional historical sites; the curio trade is rapidly depleting the forests, particularly on the Zimbabwean bank; urban migration, particularly in Victoria Falls town, presents serious health hazards.

Water, because of increased population and industrial demand, as well as global warming, has become one of the critical issues of our time. Residents at Victoria Falls, despite living on the banks of the Zambezi River, pay more for domestic water than residents anywhere else in Zimbabwe.

Already, the report notes, the offtake by the Victoria Falls North Bank Power station is reducing low-season water flow over the Eastern

Cataract to a trickle. This in turn reduces the spray over the Zambian rain forest killing vegetation and causing shrinkage of the rain forest.

The on-again, off-again, Batoka Gorge hydro-electric power project, involving a new dam and turning the gorges into a placid lake flattening out the rapids, would destroy the area's unique appeal and cost US$8 million a year in lost tourist revenue.

The World Heritage Site was set up principally for protecting and emphasising a superlative natural feature and for demonstrating an exceptional example of significant ongoing geological processes. If the Batoka Dam was built and the gorges flooded, this clear demonstration of the process of waterfall formation would be lost."

Beyond that, various biological features such as the habitat in the gorges for raptors, particularly the Taita Falcon, would be endangered, the fish population would change with slow moving water replacing fast moving, and Stone Age sites would be threatened and submerged.

The report recommends severely limiting tourist accomodation expansion at Victoria Falls town, promoting low-volume, high-value (as opposed to backpacker) tourism, considering the Falls to be a shared heritage, and drawing up a development master plan for the area.

Whether the cash-strapped Zambian and Zimbabwean governments are listening is debateable. At a subsequent meeting at Victoria Falls, a

---

### Our Common Heritage

Had each visitor to Victoria Falls last year picked a flower or a leaf weighing only five grams some 2,500 kg of rain forest would have been lost. Had they all carved their initials on a tree the whole mature rain forest would be defaced and condemned to an early death.

Conversely had each visitor picked up a piece of litter weighing only ten grams then around five tonnes of litter would have been removed from Victoria Falls last year.

Victoria Falls is a World Heritage Site meaning it belongs to everyone, not just Zimbabwe. Thus we all have a responsibility in preserving it.

So please do not remove rocks, plants, wood, or flowers, stick to designated paths of the rain forest, help clear and not create litter, prevent fires, do not deface trees.

That way you will help preserve Victoria Falls for your grandchildren's grandchildren and those who come long after.

Zambian minister interrupted a Zimbabwean's speech opposing the locating of five large tourist hotels on the Zambian bank of the river.

The minister led the participants onto a balcony and asked them to look across the river at the Elephant Hills Inter-Continental Victoria Falls rearing above the landscape. Having made his point he boarded his jet and flew back to Lusaka.

The Elephant Hills Inter-Continental is visible from the river and land.

While one can understand his irritation with the Zimbabwean speaker, that obscures the real issue. The issue is how to preserve Victoria Falls for everyone, now and in the future.

With tourism to Victoria Falls projected as tripling in the next decade, maybe the answer lies with the tourists themselves. Seventy per cent of those questioned by the IUCN researchers said they would not return to the Falls if the wilderness value were lost. That is the sort of language — hitting them below the budget-line — that governments are hopefully likely to hear and act upon.

In the meantime Zambia looks enviously at Zimbabwe, while Zibabwe perceives advice to halt development on its side of Victoria Falls as a "white plot" aimed at perpetuating the white control of the facilities.

# ZAMBEZI NATIONAL PARK

With such alternative wildlife destinations as Hwange, Matusadona, Mana Pools and Gonarezhou, coupled with the Falls themselves and their adrenalin-rush adventures, the tranquil fauna and flora of the Zambezi National Park receives scant attention.

Only about 20 per cent of visitors to Victoria Falls even visit the Zambezi National Park and even fewer visit the Mosi-oa-Tunya National Park on the Zambian side of the river.

The 573 square km (57,000 hectare) park on the Zimbabwean side of the river was created in 1951, amalgamated with the Victoria Falls Reserve and game reserve downstream, and is now called the Zambezi National Park.

It provides sanctuary for some 30 species of large and medium-sized mammals including all the so-called Big Five: elephant, buffalo, lion, leopard and rhino.

The last elephant count put the number in the Zambezi National Park at 1,297 and the number of buffalo at 1,453. But it is the elegant, scimitar-horned, sable, numbering over 200, which makes the park well worth a visit.

Sable mother and calf.

The original Victoria Falls Park 15 km upstream, and the Victoria Falls Reserve which is the home of the rain forest, were, and theoretically still are, linked by a narrow strip of land along the riverbank.

# ADVENTURES

The number of quite daft (in my view) things one can do to excite an adrenalin rush at Victoria Falls today seems to know no bounds.

When I was about to embark on this Guide book, Mike Davis, the managing director of one adventure firm, Shearwater, whose T- shirts advertise it as "The Adrenalin Company", argued that I must experience, first-hand, whitewater rafting and bunji jumping.

No way. Even in my distant youth, such pursuits would have caused second (or more) thoughts. Today, they are definitely for others.

But fortunately for the adventure companies, there seems to be an unending stream of those who seek an adrenalin rush and who are willing to pay big bucks (or get "freebies" if they are VIPs), for the thrills.

### Bunji Jumping
Zambian Chief Makuni, dressed in full ceremonial regalia, and accompanied by his village, bunji-jumped from the Victoria Falls bridge. Twice he withdrew from the platform, shaking and pale. But, urged on by his villagers, he finally took the plunge.

I had only heard about his experience. But I personally witnessed a nun (whom I thought would have known better) take the plunge. Sister Helen Doyle, a 36-year-old white Zimbabwean nun of Irish parentage, dived from the bridge to raise money for a Bulawayo hospital. She wore jeans and a T-shirt which answers everyone's question.

Had it been a spiritual or a terrifying experience, I asked? The latter, she replied adding it had been exciting but that she would not do it again. The other nuns who had assembled - and I - wondered why she had done it in the first place.

Some 40 other people jumped that day making this a highly lucrative business. Each received a certificate basically saying they had briefly taken leave of their senses and dived 111 metres off the Victoria Falls bridge, the highest commercial jump in the world.

A New Zealand company, aptly named Kiwi Extreme (now renamed African Extreme), started the craze at Victoria Falls. The "trip" is safer than a walk in the park, they claim. But which park they are referring to is not specified.

Their brochure is worth reading whether or not you are considering taking the plunge. "Bunji jumping at

A bunji jumper "flies" towards the gorge below.

Victoria Falls means launching yourself into a 111 metre void with a rubber cord as your only lifeline. Unless you're sane there's nothing to it."

For a few seconds, the brochure says, you live beyond the frontiers of the mind. The crowd goes quiet as the starter counts 5-4-3-2-1 Bunji! Your ten-second journey in space "... will change your perceptions of life, death and the cosmos."

The Awesome Foursome — bunji, whitewater rafting, sky-diving and microlighting — is available for the thrill-seekers, and when the water is low you can try the Gruesome Twosome, a bunji-jump and then straight into a raft for the whitewater.

The Kiwis apparently got the idea from a nearby group of New Hebrides islanders whose men dive from a log platform with vines tied to their ankles. Surely there must be some other way of proving one's manhood?

## Whitewater Rafting
In comparison to bunji-jumping this is a sedate pursuit. If you are over 16 years, are fit, don't have a dicky heart, don't suffer from asthma making breathing hard as you climb out of the gorge, can swim, if you are only slightly deranged, if...

If you still qualify — and want to — then what you don't need (although it may help) is previous experience unless you are planning to go on a "paddle boat", meaning you are one of the paddlers.

Gear yourself out with as little as possible. Essentials are running shoes, cork-soled yachting shoes, rubber rafting shoes, or your bare feet, a swimming costume or shorts, a T-shirt, and a liberal dose of suncream. Hats may help, but they will be washed away unless tied to your regulation-issue life-jacket.

Whitewater rafters take a dip.

If you wear glasses maybe you should leave them behind. This definitely helps avoid seeing the rapids which you may not see anyway if you're boat has over-turned or you are underwater!

Cameras, probably including underwater ones, are out unless you want to lose them at the bottom of the Zambezi River or have them damaged by spray. Anyway, the rafting companies have thought of every angle and you can buy riverbank-shot videos and still pictures from them recording your experience.

The Boiling Pot is used on the Zambian side of the river between July and January which is the low water period. In the same period the

Zimbabweans start at rapids one or four. High water is from January to the end of May or June, depending upon the rains, and in this period both Zambia and Zimbabwe start at rapid 11.

The climb out point is rapid 24 in the case of most companies. On that journey you will have navigated such aptly named rapids as Overland Truck Eater, Oblivion and Last Straw. The names of some of those above are even more graphic; Devil's Toilet Bowl, Muncher and Commercial Suicide.

While, I am assured, whitewater rafting is comparatively safe with modern equipment and skilled personnel, medical facilities, including air rescue, are on hand.

Shearwater and Frontiers, or their agents, all book whitewater rafting.

**Flight of the Angels**
A friend once remarked that as we were given two feet to walk on even horseback riding was an unnatural experience. For her the many ways of seeing Victoria Falls from the air would definitely be out.

A helicopter above the Falls.

The first of these, if you fly to Victoria Falls by commercial jet, is the arrival itself. As the pilot banks to land, the whole panorama of the Falls and the gorges is laid out before you.

For those who want a closer view — and 20 per cent of visitors to Victoria Falls do — there are five types of flights.

These include a sea or float plane which takes off from the river upstream of the Falls, helicopters, small fixed-wing planes, microlights and ultralights. It is simply a matter of availability, taste, cost, and a strong stomach.

Fixed-wing and helicopter flights over the Falls can be booked with United Air Charters and Southern Cross Aviation, float planes with Seaplane Safaris, open-cockpit, piloted Pegasus XL microlights with Batoka Sky, and ultralights with Bush Birds Flying Safaris. Alternatively you can book through your travel agent.

These flights offer good photo opportunities of Victoria Falls and the gorges. You are advised to have a new film in your camera and use a Standard 50 mm lense to obtain the best results. Camera-shake is only human.

### Skydiving
One of the Falls latest adrenalin charges. You can do a full day static line course and jump the same day from 3,000 feet, or do a 30 second tandem skydive from 8,000 feet. Probably just enough time to get married if you say the words quickly and don't pause to promise undying love and obedience!

### River-Boarding
Yet another new innovation. First of all you must be able to swim. Then you have to undergo special training with definite skill progression to prepare you to walk (or surf) three km of the Zambezi River through rapids 1 to 4, or 11 to 13 at very low and very high water respectively.

Training takes place at the Boiling Pot with the Falls as the backdrop. Here you are taught to become comfortable with the board and flippers, and develop good kicking skills.

Once your instructors feel you have the necessary skills the rapids beckon. First a raft goes through the rapid, waiting below to pick you all up. Then the guide in front chooses the safest course and the rear guard mops up. Then comes a breather, more training, and the next rapid.

What you are in fact doing is surfing on standing, instead of moving, waves. It can be a bit disorientating at first and the surfer gets the impression of incredible speed. Rapid 4 — a Grade 4 — is the toughest and only those who have shown the required skills on the first three are allowed to attempt it.

For the more sedentary who prefer their adrenalin rushes in smaller doses, there are still plentiful adventures left at Victoria Falls and in the Zambezi River.

### Booze Cruise
Its not all that it sounds, but you won't go short of liquid. Good game and bird viewing, and languid sunsets. Frontiers Adventures operates five boats offering breakfast, lunch, sunset and private hire cruises.

A Frontiers double-decker boat take visitors on an evening cruise above the Falls.

### Canoeing
The stretch above the Falls is one of the most pleasant parts of the river. You might get a minor adrenalin buzz from negotiating the mild rapids or removing yourself from the parish of a grumpy hippo whose domain you have paddled into. But mainly this is a nature outing.

The slow-moving current will push you along and your efforts are directed towards the course you choose and not survival. Birdlife

A canoeist shoots the rapids.

abounds along the river, animals occur on the banks, and the vegetation is rich and varied.

Two-person Canadian-style canoes and inflatable canoes are commonly used and bookings can be made through many companies including Shearwater and Frontiers Adventures on the Zimbabwean side of the river, and Makora Quest in Zambia which offers two-day trips with an overnight stop at a basic but comfortable riverbank camp.

### Fishing

Over 80 species of fish have been identified in the Upper Zambezi with tiger being the most exciting to catch. National Parks has fishing camps to rent at Kandahar and Mpala Jena for those with their own equipment, and various other companies, including Frontiers Adventures, provide boats, guides and tackle.

### Horseback riding

This is an unusual and very rewarding way of game viewing. Zambezi Horse Trails provide horses for scenic trail rides and bookings can be made through Shearwater.

### Elephant rides

This is another novel, highly placed, way of game viewing. In 1984, a Zimbabwean tobacco farmer and conservationist, Rory Hensman, acquired two young elephants, Miss Ellie and Jumbo, whose parents had been culled in the Zambezi Valley. Later they were joined by two Hwange orphans, Jock and Jack, whose parents had died in similar circumstances.

Hensman taught the elephants simple commands and used them instead of horses to round up cattle. But three years on they had outgrown the farm and were transferred to Jijima, a lodge in Hwange National Park, run by Wild Horizons.

*Jumbo concentrates on a drink ignoring his riders.*

They came under the tutelage of John Nicholson, a 22-year-old guide. In 1993 the elephants were translocated again, this time to Wild Horizons' Elephant Camp, a private estate 15 miles from Victoria Falls on the edge of the Zambezi National Park.

Elephant Camp deliberately sleeps only four visitors at a time and four other elephants may be booked through their town office by visitors who have come to regard a rolling journey on one of these behemoths as the highlight of an African safari.

The elephants are still young, their future uncertain. Their behaviour when they become sexually active remains unpredictable. Meanwhile, visitors watch their training and get closer to wildlife on their backs with a Zimbabwean "mahout" than they ever would by vehicle or on foot.

**Walking Safaris**

Zimbabwean guides are examined to the highest standards in Africa, and a guide is compulsory on a walking safari in a National Park. These guides are examined in every aspect of the wild including birds, butterflies and trees, and the knowledge they can impart makes such a walk very worthwhile. The guides are armed for the visitors' protection but will only use their weapons in extreme circumstances. Shearwater and several other companies do daily walks.

**Golf**

Victoria Falls area has only one golf course, in the grounds of the Elephant Hills Hotel. But this lush, Bermuda grass course, set on the bank of the Zambezi River just upstream from the Falls, contains some very special hazards.

High among them, and indicated by signs beside the water on 10th and 18th holes, is a warning to Beware of Crocodiles. They should be taken very seriously. Recently, a four-foot crocodile capable of doing considerable damage, chased an unwary caddie.

Wildlife is common. Warthogs graze, totally ignoring the golfers irrespective of whether they have played a good or bad shot.

A grazing warthog.

So common are warthogs that they merit a special citation. "Through the green, warthog damage may be treated as Ground Under Repair, with relief obtained under Rule 25-2 (b)".

Set just 980 metres above sea level, the maximum temperature is normally 25 to 30 degrees C (in October/November it rises to the lower 40 degrees C). The course is open to hotel residents and non-residents between first light, around 6.30 a.m. until last light, around 6 p.m.

There is a Halfway House where, naturally, Zambezi lager is recommended. Hole names leave no doubt that the golfer is in Africa, although, from the 12th to the 15th inclusive, one plays through Zimbabwe's version of the Bermuda Triangle.

The following hole-by-hole course description played off the men's tees is compiled by resident professional, Richard "Butch" Atkins.

1. Kudu Run. Fairly narrow fairway with bunkers on both sides, 413 m, par 4, stroke 2.

2. Charlie's Pond. No hazards apart from the pond, 150 m, par 3, stroke 18.

3. Hippo Marsh. Marsh on left, bunker guarding green, 358 m, par 4, stroke 6.

4. Elephant Walk. Needs a good tee shot and beware of bunker guarding front right of green, 497 m, par 5. stroke 8.

5. Thorn Trees. Acacia trees in line of tee shot, bunkers left and right of green, water in front, 185, par 3, stroke 10.

6. Antbear Alley. Baobab tree on left of fairway, shallow bunker in front of green, water behind, 377 m, par 4, stroke 4.

7. Buffalo Wallow. Easiest hole on the course, 326 m, par 4, stroke 16.

8. Hammerkop Roost. Tight fairway with serious water hazard on left of green, 322 m, par 4, stroke 14.

9. Goose Pan. Long water hazard left of fairway, bunkers around blind green, 482 m, par 5, stroke 12.

10. Warthog's Walk. Very tight fairway dog-legging into bunker- guarded green, 486 m, par 5, stroke 11.

11. Little Marula. Easy short hole if you miss bunkers in front of and behind green, 133 m, par 3, stroke 17.

12. Baboon's Haven. You now enter the Bermuda Triangle with fairway tree and bunker, three-tier green with bunkers beside, 357 m, par 4, stroke 9.

13. Impala Bend. Tight fairway best approached with middle iron, green bunkers, 340 m, par 4, stroke 7.

14. Rippling Water. Another tight tee shot along right-hand side water, slight dog-leg right, bunker to right of green, ("Possibly the most interesting hole," Atkins says!) 351 m, par 4, stroke 3.

15. The Baobab. Prettiest hole on course with ancient baobab and water, takes you out of the Bermuda Triangle, 159 m, par 3, stroke 15.

16. Guinea-fowl Run. A tough hole with a deep bunker (The Hole of Calcutta) on right off green, 416 m, par 4, stroke 1.

17. Water Buck Way. Easier, wide fairway but second shot into green blind with bunkers and water, 470 m, par 5, stroke 13.

18. Lion's Claw. A definite tweak in the tail with water right of fairway and blind green, 383 m, par 4, stroke 5.

# MAMMALS

A visiting British chicken farmer once asked a Zimbabwean ornithologist what the most common bird was in the country. After a brief pause, and without knowing the visitor's occupation, the Zimbabwean replied, "chickens!" Equally the most common mammals at Victoria Falls are humans.

While both those statements are true, Victoria Falls area also has about 30 other large and medium-sized mammal species plus innumerable smaller ones.

Several family herds of elephants live in the Zambezi National Park and regularly wade across the river to the islands and Zambian bank where they destroy crops in Chief Makuni's area. An insight into their awesomely destructive powers can be seen during a stroll along the river banks.

Large herds of buffalo can also be found in the Zambezi National Park although they are not as widespread as they were in the days when Thomas Baines painted them on the edge of the rain forest.

Many schools of hippo occur from just upstream of the Falls (a few have been washed over them), as far as Kazungula although it is said their numbers have diminished. Six white rhino have been introduced into the *Mosi-oa-Tunya* National Park on the Zambian side and dehorned to protect them from poachers.

Various species of antelope including waterbuck, roan, kudu, bushbuck, impala, reedbuck, eland, common duiker, steenbok, Sharpe's grysbok, klipspringer and sable may all be seen, with the latter fairly common in the Zambezi National Park. Wildebeest, giraffe, zebra, warthog and bushpig, also exist.

Lion and leopard are occasionally seen while sightings of cheetah and wild dog are rarer. The baboons you will see are known as chacma and they and vervet monkeys are common.

A maned lion.

Mammal presence tends to be much higher on the Zimbabwean side of the river, with those protected on the Zambian bank being restricted to a small area within the *Mosi-oa-Tunya* National Park which was designated primarily to protect the Falls and river area.

The distribution of mammals tends to be determined by vegetation and land usage. They also move instinctively into areas where they are protected. About 70 per cent of the Zimbabwean side of the area is under wildlife protection whereas on the Zambian side land is earmarked for commercial use and communal lands.

# BIRDS

A total of 400 species of woodland and water birds have been recorded in the Victoria Falls area, including Kazungula, and of these about 100 are water birds.

The area encompasses three distinct avian habitats, the gorges, riverine areas, and the woodland areas. In the first two 15 of the 23 bird species protected by law in Zimbabwe are to be found.

A Fish Eagle stands over the remains of a fish.

### Gorges
The most significant ornithological species found in this area are the birds of prey with 36 species living in the Batoka Gorge system of which 13 breed in the area and 16 are specially protected.

These include the rare Taita Falcon, its main known concentration being in this area. It has a black head with reddish-brown patches on the nape of its neck, a white throat, reddish-brown front, and is about one-third of a metre in length. They live solitarily or in pairs on cliffs surrounded by mature woodland, lay three to four brown eggs in a cliff basalt pot-hole, hunt smaller birds at high speed, and make a noisy, repititous "kek" alarm call.

With a 2.3 metre wingspan, jet black body except for a white back and V on the shoulders, the Black Eagle is unmistakeble. It is the second largest eagle, the Martial Eagle being shorter but heavier. The Black Eagle lives in rocky areas like the gorges where it mainly eats dassie (rock hyrax). There is concern about disturbance of the nests by ornithologists who flock to the area for sightings of the rare species.

### Riverine areas

Concern is also being expressed about a number of species in this habitat. One, the Blackcheeked Lovebird, is especially rare. The African Finfoot, Eygptian and Knobbilled Geese, and the common African Skimmer, all appear to be disturbed by the influx of tourist

Your tern. In fact a Greyheaded Gull.

boats. Birds on the islands and in the riverine swamps also seem to be similarly disturbed by human encroachment.

### Woodland areas

Bird life here seems to have adapted itself more to the growing numbers of visitors but the drone through daylight hours of planes is a matter of concern.

Overall the impression from ringing counts is that the numbers of water-based birds and warblers is in decline due to drought, bush clearance and general disturbance.

# REPTILES

The comparative absence of crocodiles at Victoria Falls will trouble few visitors. The closest you are likely to get to them is via the crocodile cocktail on your hotel menu or at the crocodile farm.

The python is the largest snake found at Victoria Falls. Four-fifths of the other snakes in the area are non-venomous and even those that are dangerous prefer to avoid humans.

What you are much more likely to see are terrapins, tortoises, lizards, agamas, skinks (also lizards), chameleons, amphisbaenidaes (small burrowing, limbless reptiles), frogs and toads.

Two types of tortoises, the Leopard and the Hinged, are found at the Falls. The former mainly eats grass, the latter eats vegetable matter as well as snails, millipedes and carrion.

A Nile Monitor lizard.

Four types of lizards or geckos are found in the area. These are the Tropical House, Cape Dwarf, Chobe Dwarf and O'Shaughnessy's Banded. All may be found on tree trunks or on house walls.

The Nile Monitor or Water Leguaan is very common on the Zambezi and is the largest African lizard growing to two-and-a-half feet in length. Its whiplash tail is a powerful defence weapon.

Frogs and toads, even if you do not see them, will make themselves heard. There are five species of toads and 11 of frogs with such bizarre names as Band Rubber Frog, Natal Puddle Frog and Marble Pig-snouted Frog. Some are brilliantly coloured and well worth photographing.

# FISH

Victoria Falls, not surprisingly, is a major barrier to fish movement between the Middle and Upper Zambezi. A total of 84 species are found above the Falls compared to 64 below them. Of these only 30 species are common to both areas.

The Zambezi River has been divided into six distinct zones with 360 fish species recorded along the river. This is comparable to the Nile and only beaten by the Congo River where over 600 species have been recorded.

Wild Date Palms cast their reflection in the Zambezi River.

In the Zambezi, in common with all rivers, the fish at the source are small allowing them to hide from predators. They are also adapted for colder temperatures and faster flowing water.

As the river progresses forming deeper water the fish become bigger until, finally, at the mouth of the river one encounters larger ocean fish such as sharks.

So, basically, the bigger the river the larger the fish and the greater the number of species.

Of the 84 species of fish found above the Falls, only about three-quarters of them occur in the area you will be visiting. And of these 60-odd some are more notable than others.

Largely because of sports fishermen and because of the fight it puts up, the Tiger is the best known species among visitors along the Zambezi River, including above Victoria Falls.

The one found in the Zambezi is the southernmost of four species, with the Goliath Tiger caught in the Congo River weighing three times as much.

Throughout the year Tiger can be caught on bait or lure, with the best fishing coming at the end of the rainy season (May/June) and in the hotter months (October/January).

Another prize-fighter among fish is the African Pike. This exists above, but not below, the Falls.

A total of 35 species of Barbs and Yellowfish are found in the area and some fishermen argue that the Yellowfish is a better fighter than the legendary Tiger.

The Vundu, only found below the Falls, is the river's heavyweight champion, a 50 kg fish having been landed, and if anglers are to be believed, it is only a matter of time before that record is broken.

Next heaviest is the Sharp-toothed Catfish and the record for this is 30.8 kg — but that was in 1947. More usually they weigh in at around 17 kg.

They exist on both sides of the Falls, are scavengers, and can often be found below herons' nests waiting for young to fall out.

Some fish, like Electric Barbels, can give the unsuspecting a nasty shock. Minnows control mosquitoes by eating their larvae. Some fish are aquarium species, and some of the 17 species of bream make the best eating.

# BUTTERFLIES & INSECTS

The hot, dry savannah and mopane woodland of the area, together with the Zambezi River, its variations in mood and tempo, and the rain forest, all combine to create a wide and varied habitat for butterflies and insects.

There are 70 to 80 butterfly species in the Victoria Falls area and several hundred moths. The most noticeable butterflies are the Swallowtails, some with, and some without, tails. Among the Whites one of the most common at the Falls is the delicate pale blue Cambridge Vagrant.

Damselflies (a sub-group of dragonflies), with their widely separated eyes distinguishing them from dragonflies, are well represented.

But it is the habits of damselflies and dragonflies which are most interesting. They are predators on other insects and can fly backwards. You may have seen them skimming and dipping across quiet water and assumed they were hunting insects.

In fact it was the females laying

A rare photograph of an Eared Commodore (*Precis tugela*).

A common Mother of Pearl (Protogoniomorpha parhassus).

eggs gently on the surface. The eggs then drift to the bottom, hatching after a few days. But it is the act of copulation which is both remarkable and acrobatic. Most insects breed much like humans. But Odonata, as the insect is formally known, pursue a much more circuitous route.

First the male bends his abdomen forward to transfer sperm from the tip of it to a pouch under the third abdominal segment. This accomplished, he flies off in search of a female. Having found one, he clasps her behind the head and she completes the elaborate process by bending her abdomen forward to make contact with the deposited male sperm. Then they fly around in tandem. Errol Flynn would have loved it!

Stoneflies, mayflies, some 50 species of grasshoppers and crickets, whose colours make them hard to see when they remain still in their habitat, cockroaches, praying mantises, stick insects, earwigs, ants, beetles and bugs (which is a scientific term to include such intruders as bedbugs), all occur in the area.

# TREES & SHRUBS

Victoria Falls vegetation is dictated by its altitude (915 metres above sea-level), hot climate, humidity, limited rainfall (600- 700 millimetres a year), and the geological composition.

The basalt base is shallow and supports mopane woodland or mixed mopane scrub. The Kalahari Sands are dominated by miombo / Kalahari woodland, featuring trees such as *umkusu* or *gusu* (in the past used for railway sleepers and parquet tiles), brachystegia and African ordeal trees.

The river itself, like many rivers, has a fringe of riverine vegetation. This is a very narrow belt, at most 100 metres wide, and includes the rain forest which, in reality, is a riverine forest as opposed to a tropical or montane forest.

In the rain forest, so called because of the spray from the Falls, over 400 plant species have been identified.

African ebony is one the most trees in the rain forest. The straight trunk is black barked and the trees bear yellow hard-skinned, plum-like, fruit, which are edible. Of the four fig trees, the broom-cluster fig is recognisable by its edible fig-size fruit growing in clusters on the trunk, while strangler figs do their self-evident job slowly throttling their host trees.

Waterberry trees bear white eucalyptus-styled flowers, and *musikiri* has a fruit which looks like a wooden, half-peeled banana. The wild olive has fruit making it easily reognisable and wild date palms are common.

It is among the 150 herbaceous species that one finds the main rarities. Fireballs shine in the undergrowth in November at the start of the rains, ground orchids bear distinctive white flowers and flame lilies with their bright red and yellow flowers, stand out.

Tropical creepers, or lianas, are visible in several places on the edges of the rain forest while wild date palms are more prominent in the area known as the Palm Grove.

# WHERE TO STAY

Victoria Falls hotels, like those throughout Zimbabwe and much of the world, are rated on the one to five international star system. In Zimbabwe's case this seems totally illogical. Maybe in Europe or North America you want a telephone, television and a radio in your room. But is that really what you want in Africa? Maybe you do.

Most if not all hotels are air-conditioned, ensuite, and so on, and they have swimming pools, tennis courts, bars, restaurants with medium quality cuisines (a common feature in many Zimbabwean hotels), plus all sorts of other etcs. Only where it merits are any of these extras mentioned. And if I wanted to visit a casino I would go to Monte Carlo.

Lodges are smaller and away from the hubbub of Victoria Falls town. The food and decor are generally preferable for those who seek greater privacy, a pristine environment, ceiling fans, mosquito nets and a touch of yesteryear — and they still have the Falls and its adventures on the doorstep.

## ZIMBABWE

### Hotels and Lodges

### Victoria Falls Safari Lodge
[PO Box 29, Victoria Falls, Tel (113) 3201-4, Fax (113) 3205]
This is my favourite place to stay at Victoria Falls for several reasons. The first is my pocket. Secondly, one can choose between the thatched, self-catering Lokuthula Lodges (with warthog, vervet monkey and banded mongoose as regular visitors), which are very comfortable, have outside dining, and sleep six or eight, or the wood-and-thatch main hotel overlooking an active and busy waterhole. Thirdly, the food in the main hotel dining room is unusually good for the safari circuit. Fourthly, its location and design shows environmental thought. Finally, there are no TV and radios in the rooms. The Lodge faces due west making it an ideal spot for photography.

The Victoria Falls Safari Lodge thatched structures reflected in its waterhole.

### The Victoria Falls Hotel

[PO Box 10, Victoria Falls, Tel (113) 4203/4751, Fax (113) 4586]
If for no other reason than that it was the first hotel (built 1904), and is steeped in history, this grand establishment merits special mention. But there is much more reason than that. The spray from the Falls can be seen from the terrace and lawns, and the bridge and the second gorge are right in front. Refurbished again, it now has 182 rooms and is rated as one of the world's 25 most famous hotels.

Early picture of The Victoria Falls Hotel.

### Elephant Hills Inter-Continental Victoria Falls
[PO Box 300, Victoria Falls, Tel (113) 4793, Fax (113) 4655]
This hotel was re-built as a "retreat" for Commonwealth leaders during their summit in Zimbabwe in 1991. Facilities have been upgraded to meet Inter-Continental standards. Overlooks an excellent golf course, the Zambezi River and Falls to the east.

### Makasa Sun Hotel
[PO Box 90, Victoria Falls, Tel (113) 4275, Fax (113) 4782]
Located across the street next to The Victoria Falls Hotel, and also run by Zimbabwe Sun Hotels, this hotel has a casino. It also has conference facilities for 200 and it has a seafood restaurant on the roof overlooking the Falls.

The Victoria Falls Hotel.

### Gorges
[PO Box 2914, Harare, Tel (4) 796982/796990/1 Fax (4) 796989]
Located 23.5 km from Victoria Falls perched high above the gorges, this hotel is managed by Block Lodges who run a number of notable hotels in Kenya and Zimbabwe. The stone-under-thatch suites have their own balconies providing magnificent views of rapids 19 and 20 of the

Zambezi River below the Falls.  Excellent bird watching of rare species.  Young children are not permitted.

## Imbabala Safari Camp
[PO Box 159, Victoria Falls, Tel (113) 2004/4219, Fax (113) 4349]
Located on a small private concession, this camp is on the banks of the Zambezi River.  Imbabala offers the chance to relax, view game, birds, fish and visit Chobe National Park in Botswana with some of the area's most experienced guides. Accommodation in A-frame chalets with electricity, fans and mosquito nets.  All have views of the river.

## Elephant Camp
Details same as Imbabala
Situated 25-km from Victoria Falls on a 35,000-acre privately owned wildlife estate, this camp offers a special experience.  Not only can wildlife be viewed from the back of an elephant (which means you get closer than on foot or in a vehicle), but the visitor also shares a day in the life of elephants — Miss Ellie, Jumbo, Jock and Jack — at close quarters.  The camp accommodates a maximum of eight guests in four ensuite chalets with electricity, fans and mosquito nets.

## Masuwe Lodge
[PO Box 257, Victoria Falls, Tel (113) 4699, Fax (14) 708119]
Another excellent small lodge on a 1,000-acre private wildlife estate adjacent to Zambezi National Park.  Accomodation in ten tents on stilts under thatch, each with a teak viewing platform over floodlit waterhole.  Owned by Landela, it has excellent food, a growing reputation, and won the Victoria Falls Publicity Association best lodge award in 1996.

## Sekuti's Drift
[PO Box 257, Victoria Falls, Tel (113) 426524, Fax (14) 708119]
This is the second Victoria Falls facility (the first being Masuwe) of Zimbabwe's most upmarket operator, Landela, which is an Ndebele word meaning "track".  Fifteen minutes from Victoria Falls, Sekuti's warm and unpretensious architecture and decor adds grace to the sparse colonial style of a century ago.

## Operators

## Shearwater Adventures
[PO Box 125, Victoria Falls, Tel (113) 4471/4648, Fax (113) 4341]
Victoria Falls largest group of companies advertises itself as *"The Andrenalin Company"* and given their vast range of activities including bunji jumping, whitewater rafting, river-boarding, canoeing, helicopter

flights, micro-lighting and bookings for almost every other adventure they are bound to give you a buzz.

## United Touring Company
[PO Box 35, Victoria Falls, Tel (113) 4267, Fax (113) 3306/4225]
This international group covers the whole of Zimbabwe offering a wide range of services such as car hire, airport and hotel transfers, river cruises, touring and game flights. Hertz and Frontiers Adventures are part of the group thereby expanding the range on offer.

## Dabula Safaris
[PO Box 210, Victoria Falls, Tel (113) 4453/4481, Fax (113) 4609]
Activities include airport/hotel transfers, Botswana and Zambia transfers, guided tours of the Falls, craft village and crocodile farm, three - hour and full-day game drives and walks in the Zambezi National Park, lunch and sunset cruises, specialist birding and fishing, rafting and scenic flights over the Falls.

## Cultural tourism.

This is a fairly new concept in tourism in Africa and too often it is anything but authentic. Rent-a-village or a dance troupe is an often tokenistic way of trotting out supposed locals to round-off the visitors African experience.

Monde village, located 14-km from Victoria Falls town, offers as near as you will get to the real — not reconstructed — African environment.

A joint venture between Baobab Safaris in Victoria Falls and the Monde village community, the visit centres around Melusi Ndlovu who lives in the village where he leads a subsistence life with his wife Savee and their children.

But he has travelled much further than most of his fellow villagers. During the Southern Rhodesian independence war he was a freedom fighter and today is still referred to by his war *(chimurenga)* name *mpisi* which means hyena.

During the years he was based in neighbouring Zambia he travelled to the Eastern bloc countries for specialist training. This exposed him to new cultures while sharpening his respect for his own.

He is Ndebele and his childhood was steeped in the culture of that tribe. He was instructed by his grandfather, a noted traditional healer (not to be confused with witchdoctor), and his father, Chief Marathusa.

A Nambian hut in Monde village.

Today Mpisi is a respected traditional healer in his own right and one of the leaders of Monde village. He is proud of his roots and concerned about the disintegration of Zimbabwe culture. Visitors, he feels, should learn about the country's history and culture —as well as seeing Victoria Falls and the wildlife.

In 1996 the Monde Village Development Committee established a trust fund through which the whole community benefits from visitors. Only genuine villagers are involved in showing visitors around while Baobab Safaris is responsible for marketing and transporting visitors.

There is none of the usual sensational hype. Rather visitors are given an authentic depiction of Zimbabwean rural life, warts and all.

The history of the Ndebele and Nambian people who live in the village is explained, homes are visited, indigenous food and drinks are shared, production methods can be seen in the fields, the importance of religion and customs is discussed with spiritual leaders, and a traditional healer shares the secrets of his herbal cures with the visitor.

In addition Babobab Safaris offer a village tour with dinner and a full-day cultural tour combined with a river cruise and lunch followed by a game drive.

## FACILITIES

From being a fairly poorly supplied village, Victoria Falls has grown by leaps and bounds in the last decade to cope with the tourist influx. Most places take credit cards and travellers' cheques, and there are banks, chemists, supermarkets and much more to look after your necessities. Specifically tourist related places of interest and general information follow below.

### Curio Shops

The first curio dealer in the Victoria Falls area was almost certainly King Lewanika, the Lozi leader. By 1905 the annual income from his curio shop in Livingstone was said to be £200, a large amount in those days.

King Lewanika.

The earliest issues of *The Livingstone Mail* in 1906 carried advertisements for curios. The following year the customer and the trade were described in some detail by the same newspaper. Special trains arriving from South Africa's Cape Colony were carrying almost 400 "excursionists". Their two-hour visit to Livingstone "...was a sight to be remembered."

"Every store displaying curios did a roaring trade and the visitors were surrounded by an odoriferous crowd of assorted natives, offering for sale anything between a spear and a handful of kaffir oranges; the prices they demanded were enough to take one's breath away, but in many cases they got them."

Curio selling appears to have come to Victoria Falls town slightly later. Percy Clark, probably noting King Lewanika's success, and with an eye to the future, opened shop in 1903. Jack Soper, who had arrived at the Falls as toll-keeper on the bridge, opened in 1910. His shop remains today and is probably the best stocked in the Craft Village just off the town centre. "Fred" Forest is the Craft Village's personality and traditional dances are performed on the premises. The Jairos Jiri shop has a good range of basketware while Studio Africana has artefacts from all over the continent. Elsewhere there are curio shops at hotels and throughout Victoria Falls and the curio stall on the Zambian side, while slightly more expensive, is different and well worth a visit.

Confronted with such an array of curios, plus demanding curio carvers and sellers, how does the visitor decide what to buy. Indeed, as a Norwegian expert once asked, "What is a curio?" One answer to that seems to be something "novel, rare or bizarre." Another might be something "primitive" reflecting the European perception of the culture and tradition of the area. The following gives you some guidance as to what is authentic, or closer to, at the Falls.

Ever-larger carvings of giraffe are sold by roadside curio sellers.

## Choosing a carving

The majority of the Falls carvers are Luvale, Luchazi, Mbunda, Lozi and Leya. The first three come from Zambia's Northwestern Province and are collectively called the Lunda-Luvale people. The Lozi come from Zambia's Western Province and the Leya traditionally inhabited the Livingstone area.

The Lozi, given Lewanika's curio shop and other evidence, were probably the first curio producers. Their work, like that of the Leya, is primarily utilitarian and made from hardwood. The Lunda-Luvale, whose work has been described as "both profane and religious", prefer the greater flexibility of softwood and their work is richer and more varied.

The Lunda-Luvale use painted masks of barkcloth and wood in boys' initiation rites, while scenes from rural life and geometric designs decorate walking sticks, stools, musical instruments and calabashes. The Lozi and Leya tend to specialise in animal carving.

Some animal carvings such as elephants, rhino, hippo, crocodiles and tortoises appear to have local traditional origins. Others, such as the popular and ever-larger giraffe carvings along the roadside, are more obscure. Like much else, including some masks at the Falls, they probably had their origins in East Africa or Zaire.

The traditional masks were simpler, and generally smaller, than the modern ones. The most usual ones were almost entirely undecorated on the face with a large hair-top above. Their origins are thought to come from the Lunda-Luvale initiation ceremony mask known as *Nalindele* or *Mwana Pwo*. Today they are much decorated and coloured.

Drums are a Lunda-Luvale speciality. But todays drums are shorter and wider, more decorated, painted and exaggerated, than the earlier traditional drums which were made from hardwood and were therefore less easily transported by the visitor.

The likelihood is you will find very little which is authentic and traditional. But among items traditional to the area, particularly those produced by Lunda-Luvale carvers, distant roots lurk below the surface. Among Lunda-Luvale carvers look for items related to ritual purposes; among the Lozi and the Leya carvers for utilarian items such as ornate wooden dishes and stools.

Always remember that what is on offer has rarely been made to serve a traditional or utilitarian purpose. It has been conceived and crafted for strangers like you. You may think the carvings "primitive". That is what the seller is bargaining on. At the end of the day it is all about supply and demand.

## Restaurants

The open-air Boma restaurant (part of the Victoria Falls Safari Lodge complex), with a swimming pool and bar, is one of the local favourites. Food includes antelope, crocodile and ostrich you may see wild in the bush, as well as more authentic African dishes. The Cattleman is a steak house where the Wild West theme at Victoria Falls is quite inappropriate. But the food is good. Explorers has television blaring (usually sport), live music at night, moderate food, and is usually full. The next door Pizza Bistro is ordinary and there are the usual take-away and fast-food joints such as Wimpy.

## Medical advice

Victoria Falls is in a malaria zone so ensure you take a prophylaxis. Consult your local doctor and start the course before you arrive and continue it for six weeks after you leave. For those who don't find them claustrophobic, mosquito nets are usually provided, and insect repellants, long-sleeved shirts and trousers are advisable at night.

Minor ailments can be treated at the local hospital and there is a resident private general practitioner. For serious cases which cannot be dealt with locally, the Medical Air Rescue Service (MARS) is on call 24 hours a day and most safari organisations have medical cover allowing evacuation. Check that the organisation you may choose to go with is covered.

Bilhartzia — and crocodiles — occur in the slower moving water and swimming is not advisable. They are not present in the fast gorge waters below the pools so whitewater rafters do not have to contend with these particular hazards. Tap water is treated and generally quite safe in the main hotels. But it is in limited supply because of Victoria Falls' ancient pumps. Do not drink water directly from the river although rafters may inadvertently swallow some.

## Photography

Most photographic requirements, inluding batteries, are available in Zimbabwe. But, if you are going to Zambia, or have requirements beyond the basics, you are advised to carry supplies with you. One-hour processing of colour negatives is available at Victoria Falls, but slides have to be sent elsewhere and you will be better advised to wait until you return home before processing them.

There is often a double rainbow at Devil's Cataract at mid-morning making this a good time for pictures. Viewpoints 2 to 4 offer good frontal picture opportunities. Sunset, with a red orb behind and reflections on the water, is another good shot.

The best pictures of the Main Falls in all their splendour with 500,000 litres of water a second pouring over them, is in June/July. Danger Point is best late in the day and the Zambian side offers spectacular shots across the Eastern Cataract. While professionals shoot a huge number of films to get the required result, you are not in that business and just want to record your visit accurately. Apart from keeping your equipment dry one further piece of advice is to take your light readings from the sky and bracket your exposure by a stop either way. That works particularly well with sunsets and the rejected shots are well worth the expense. A tripod (or even bipod) will help with all your riverbank pictures and for aerial shots try to load new film before taking off. A high shutter speed and 50 mm standard lense should produce the best results.

## VISITING ZAMBIA

While Livingstone used to be the tourist centre for the area, this role has now shifted to Victoria Falls town in Zimbabwe. Thus, you are most likely today to be visiting Zambia from Zimbabwe and there are various ways of doing so.

You can cross the Falls bridge to Zambia on foot, by bike, bus, car or train. Whichever you choose you have to go through Customs and Immigration on either side of the bridge so you need your passport.

Your personal effects can be imported duty free and entering Zambia you are allowed 200 cigarettes, a litre of wine and a litre of spirits. Zimbabwe's allowance is more generous, five litres of alcohol, of which two litres may be spirits.

Temporary import permits for vehicles can be obtained at the border free of charge, but taking hire vehicles across the bridge is a hassle bordering on the impossible. Check this with the hiring company.

Visas are required for many nationalities. Zambia recently introduced visas for British subjects in retaliation for Britain introducing visa requirement for Zambians. As the largest number of visitors to Zimbabwe from outside the continent are British, this policy is likely to backfire with British visitors choosing not to pay the US$50 visa fee.

## CHECKLIST OF THE MAIN MAMMALS OF VICTORIA FALLS

The visitor should note that only the main large-sized and medium-sized mammals are included. Many other smaller animals, such as mongoose, otters, squirrels and genets, exist in the area.

Elephant
Buffalo
Hippopotamus
Giraffe
Eland
Sable
Roan
Kudu
Waterbuck
Zebra
White rhinoceros
Black rhinoceros
Wildebeest

Impala
Bushbuck
Reedbuck
Steenbok
Warthog
Bushpig
Baboon
Vervet monkey
Lion
Leopard
Cheetah
Spotted hyena
Blackbacked Jackel

A buffalo glowers.

# BIRD CHECK LIST FOR THE VICTORIA FALLS

All numbers used are taken from Roberts' *Birds of Southern Africa*. This list was compiled by Dr Kit Hustler of Wild Horizons, PO Box 159, Victoria Falls, Zimbabwe (Tel: 263 (13) 4219) and Mr Peter Ginn of Peter Ginn Birding Safaris, PO Box 44, Marondera, Zimbabwe (Tel/Fax: 263 (79) 23411). Please note that this is a selection of over 400 birds species recorded in the Victoria Falls area and should not be classed as a definitive list.

| No. | Bird Name | No. | Bird Name |
|-----|-----------|-----|-----------|
| 058 | Reed Cormorant | 140 | Martial Eagle |
| 060 | Darter | 142 | Brown Snake Eagle |
| 062 | Grey Heron | 143 | Blackbreasted Snake Eagle |
| 064 | Goliath Heron | 146 | Bateleur |
| 065 | Purple Heron | 148 | African Fish Eagle |
| 066 | Great White Egret | 149 | Steppe Buzzard |
| 067 | Little Egret | 154 | Lizard Buzzard |
| 068 | Yellowbilled Egret | 159 | Little Banded Goshawk |
| 069 | Black Egret | 161 | Gabar Goshawk |
| 071 | Cattle Egret | 163 | Dark Chanting Goshawk |
| 074 | Greenbacked Heron | 171 | Peregrine Falcon |
| 081 | Hamerkop | 172 | Lanner Falcon |
| 083 | White Stork | 173 | Hobby Falcon |
| 084 | Black Stork | 180 | E. Redfooted Kestrel |
| 087 | Openbill Stork | 183 | Lesser Kestrel |
| 088 | Saddlebill Stork | 188 | Coqui Francolin |
| 089 | Marabou Stork | 189 | Crested Francolin |
| 090 | Yellowbill Stork | 196 | Natal Francolin |
| 091 | Sacred Ibis | 199 | Swainson's Francolin |
| 093 | Glossy Ibis | 203 | Helmeted Guinea Fowl |
| 094 | Hadeda Ibis | 205 | Kurrichan Buttonquail |
| 095 | African Spoonbill | 213 | Black Crake |
| 099 | Whitefaced Duck | 226 | Moorhen |
| 102 | Egyptian Goose | 230 | Kori Bustard |
| 108 | Redbilled Teal | 238 | Blackbellied Korhaan |
| 114 | Pygmy Goose | 240 | African Jacana |
| 115 | Knobbilled Duck | 249 | Threebanded Plover |
| 116 | Spurwinged Goose | 255 | Crowned Plover |
| 121 | Hooded Vulture | 258 | Blacksmith Plover |
| 123 | Whitebacked Vulture | 259 | Whitecrowned Plover |
| 124 | Lappetfaced Vulture | 260 | Wattled Plover |
| 125 | Whiteheaded Vulture | 264 | Common Sandpiper |
| 126a | Yellowbilled Kite | 266 | Wood Sandpiper |
| 126b | Black Kite | 297 | Spotted Dikkop |
| 127 | Blackshouldered Kite | 298 | Water Dikkop |
| 131 | Black Eagle | 306 | Rock Pratincole |
| 132 | Tawny Eagle | 315 | Greyheaded Gull |
| 135 | Wahlberg's Eagle | 339 | Whitewinged Tern |
| 137 | African Hawk Eagle | 343 | African Skimmer |

| No. | Bird Name | No. | Bird Name |
|-----|-----------|-----|-----------|
| 352 | Redeyed Dove | 474 | Greater Honeyguide |
| 354 | Cape Turtle Dove | 476 | Lesser Honeyguide |
| 355 | Laughing Dove | 486 | Cardinal Woodpecker |
| 358 | Greenspotted Dove | 487 | Bearded Woodpecker |
| 361 | Green Pigeon | 494 | Rufousnaped Lark |
| 364 | Meyer's Parrot | 505 | Dusky Lark |
| 370 | Schalow's Lourie | 518 | European Swallow |
| 371 | Purplecrested Lourie | 520 | Whitethroated Swallow |
| 373 | Grey Lourie | 522 | Wiretailed Swallow |
| 377 | Redchested Cuckoo | 524 | Redbreasted Swallow |
| 385 | Klaas' Cuckoo | 527 | Lesserstriped Swallow |
| 386 | Diederik Cuckoo | 529 | Rock Martin |
| 390 | Senegal Coucal | 538 | Black Cuckooshrike |
| 391 | Burchell's Coucal | 541 | Forktailed Drongo |
| 394 | Wood Owl | 543 | European Golden Oriole |
| 398 | Pearlspotted Owl | 544 | African Golden Oriole |
| 399 | Barred Owl | 545 | Blackheaded Oriole |
| 401 | Spotted Eagle Owl | 548 | Pied Crow |
| 402 | Giant Eagle Owl | 554 | Southern Black Tit |
| 405 | Fierynecked Nightjar | 558 | Grey Penduline Tit |
| 412 | Black Swift | 560 | Arrowmarked Babbler |
| 417 | Little Swift | 568 | Blackeyed Bulbul |
| 421 | Palm Swift | 574 | Yellowbellied Bulbul |
| 426 | Redfaced Mousebird | 576 | Kurrichane Thrush |
| 428 | Pied Kingfisher | 580 | Groundscraper Thrush |
| 429 | Giant Kingfisher | 587 | Capped Wheatear |
| 431 | Malachite Kingfisher | 593 | Mocking Chat |
| 435 | Brownhooded Kingfisher | 599 | Heuglin's Robin |
| 437 | Striped Kingfisher | 613 | Whitebrowed Robin |
| 438 | European Bee-eater | 643 | Willow Warbler |
| 441 | Carmine Bee-eater | 648 | Yellowbreasted Apalis |
| 443 | Whitefronted Bee-eater | 651 | Longbilled Crombec |
| 444 | Little Bee-eater | 653 | Yellowbellied Eremomela |
| 447 | Lilacbreasted Roller | 657 | Bleating Warbler |
| 448 | Rackettailed Roller | 664 | Fantailed Cisticola |
| 450 | Broadbilled Roller | 683 | Tawnyflanked Prinia |
| 451 | Hoopoe | 689 | Spotted Flycatcher |
| 452 | Redbilled Woodhoopoe | 691 | Bluegrey Flycatcher |
| 454 | Scimitarbilled Woodhoopoe | 694 | Black Flycatcher |
| | | 695 | Marico Flycatcher |
| 455 | Trumpeter Hornbill | 701 | Chinspot Batis |
| 457 | Grey Hornbill | 710 | Paradise Flycatcher |
| 458 | Redbilled Hornbill | 711 | African Pied Wagtail |
| 460 | Crowned Hornbill | 713 | Cape Wagtail |
| 463 | Ground Hornbill | 733 | Redbacked Shrike |
| 464 | Blackcollared Barbet | 737 | Tropical Boubou |
| 470 | Yellowfronted Tinker Barbet | 739 | Crimsonbreasted Shrike |
| | | 740 | Puffback |

| No. | Bird Name | No. | Bird Name |
|-----|-----------|-----|-----------|
| 741 | Brubru | 807 | Thickbilled Weaver |
| 743 | Threestreaked Tchagra | 810 | Spectacled Weaver |
| 744 | Blackcrowned Tchagra | 811 | Spottedbacked Weaver |
| 748 | Orangebreasted Bush Shrike | 814 | Masked Weaver |
|     |           | 816 | Golden Weaver |
| 751 | Greyheaded Bush Shrike | 818 | Brownthroated Weaver |
| 753 | White Helmet Shrike | 819 | Redheaded Weaver |
| 754 | Redbilled Helmet Shrike | 821 | Redbilled Quelea |
| 760 | Wattled Starling | 824 | Red Bishop |
| 761 | Plumcoloured Starling | 829 | Whitewinged Widow |
| 764 | Glossy Starling | 834 | Melba Finch |
| 765 | Greater Blue-eared Starling | 841 | Jameson's Firefinch |
|     |           | 842 | Redbilled Firefinch |
| 769 | Redwinged Starling | 844 | Blue Waxbill |
| 771 | Yellowbill Oxpecker | 846 | Common Waxbill |
| 772 | Redbilled Oxpecker | 855 | Cutthroat Finch |
| 787 | Whitebellied Sunbird | 857 | Bronze Mannikin |
| 791 | Scarletchested Sunbird | 861 | Shafttailed Whydah |
| 792 | Black Sunbird | 862 | Paradise Whydah |
| 799 | Whitebrowed Sparrowweaver | 863 | Broadtailed Paradise Whydah |
|     |           | 865 | Purple Widowfinch |
| 801 | House Sparrow | 867 | Steelblue Widowfinch |
| 804 | Greyheaded Sparrow | 869 | Yelloweye Canary |
| 805 | Yellowthroated Sparrow | 884 | Goldenbreasted Bunting |

## CHECKLIST OF TREES AND SHRUBS OF VICTORIA FALLS AREA

The following checklist includes some of the more common, or more notable, trees and shrubs to be seen in and around the Victoria Falls.

For further reading, Meg Coates Palgrave's *Key to the Trees of Zimbabwe* is recommended. In addition, the "Know Your Trees" course provides unique insights. Bookings can be made direct with Meg at PO Box 4643, Harare, Zimbabwe (Tel: 263 (4) 742 765 Fax: 263 (4) 742 800).

Some Trees in and around the Rain Forest

| Tree/Shrub Name | Botanical Name |
|-----------------|----------------|
| African Mangosteen | *Garcinia livingstonei* |
| Azanza | *Azanza garckeana* |
| Batoka Plum | *Flacourtia indica* |
| Bird Plum | *Berchemia discolor* |
| Blue-Bark Commiphora | *Commiphora caerulea* |
| Broom-Cluster Fig | *Ficus sur* |
| Bush Guarri | *Euclea racemosa* |
| Carrot Tree | *Steganotaenia araliacea* |
| Common Red Milkwood | *Mimusops zeyheri* |

| Tree/Shrub Name | Botanical Name |
|---|---|
| Common Wild Fig | *Ficus thonningii* |
| Crocodile-Bark | *Diospyros quiloensis* |
| Ebony Dalbergia | *Dalbergia melanoxylon* |
| Ebony Diospyros | *Diospyros mespiliformis* |
| False Marula | *Lannea schweinfurthii* |
| Feretia | *Feretia aeruginescens* |
| Ginger-Bush | *Tetradenia riparia* |
| Grape Strychnos | *Strychnos potatorum* |
| Gummy Gardenia | *Gardenia resiniflua* |
| Kirkia | *Kirkia acuminata* |
| Knob-Thorn | *Acacia nigrescens* |
| Knobby Bridelia | *Bridelia cathartica* |
| Lavender Croton | *Croton gratissimus* |
| Leadwood | *Combretum imberbe* |
| Long-Pod Cassia | *Cassia abbreviata* |
| Lowveld Milkberry | *Manilkara mochisia* |
| Marula | *Sclerocarya birrea* |
| Monkey Thorn | *Acacia galpinii* |
| Mopane | *Colophospermum mopane* |
| Natal Mahogany | *Trichilia emetica* |
| Northern Premna | *Premna senensis* |
| Northern Dwaba-Berry | *Friesodielsia obovata* |
| Pepper-Leaved Commiphora | *Commiphora mossambicensis* |
| Pink-Fruited Canthium | *Canthium glaucum* |
| Pod Mahogany | *Afzelia quanzensis* |
| Poison-Pod Albizia | *Albizia versicolor* |
| Purple Hook-Berry | *Artabotrys brachypetalus* |
| Purple-Pod Terminalia | *Terminalia prunioides* |
| Rain-Tree | *Lonchocarpus capassa* |
| Red-Leaved Rock Fig | *Ficus ingens* |
| Red Star-Apple | *Diospyros lycioides* |
| River Climbing Acacia | *Acacia schweinfurthii* |
| Rough-Leaved Boscia | *Boscia angustifolia* |
| Rough-Leaved Croton | *Croton menyhartii* |
| Rubber Hedge | *Euphorbia tirucalli* |
| Sausage Tree | *Kigelia africana* |
| Short-Pod | *Rourea orientalis* |
| Sickle-Leaved Albizia | *Albizia harveyi* |
| Small-Leaved Bloodwood | *Pterocarpus lucens* |
| Smooth-Bark Tricalysia | *Tricalysia junodii* |
| Snowberry Tree | *Flueggea virosa* |
| Soft-Leaved Commiphora | *Commiphora mollis* |
| Spike-Thorn | *Maytenus heterophylla* |
| Tasselberry | *Antidesma venosum* |
| Tree Vernonia | *Vernonia amygdalina* |
| Velvet-leaved Combretum | *Combretum molle* |
| Wild Olive | *Olea europea* |
| Wonderboom Fig | *Ficus cordata* |

| Tree/Shrub Name | Botanical Name |
|---|---|
| Woodland Waterberry | *Syzygium guineense ssp. guineense* |
| Woodland Vepris | *Vepris reflexa* |
| Woolly Caper Bush | *Capparis tomentosa* |
| Zambezi Coca Tree | *Erythroxylum zambesiacum* |
| Zambezi Vitex | *Vitex petersiana* |
| Zambezi Waterberry | *Syzygium guineense ssp. barotsense* |
| Zig-Zag Terminalia | *Terminalia stuhlmannii* |

Palms

| | |
|---|---|
| Ilala / Vegetable Ivory Palm | *Hyphaene petersiana* |
| Wild Date Palm | *Phoenix reclinata* |

Other trees in the vicinity of Victoria Falls

| | |
|---|---|
| Burkea | *Burkea africana* |
| Albida | *Faidherbia albida* |
| Angular-Stemmed Commiphora | *Commiphora karibensis* |
| Baobab | *Adansonia digitata* |
| Batoka Diospyros | *Diospyros batocana* |
| Blue-Bark Commiphora | *Commiphora caerulea* |
| Commiphora Rhus | *Rhus tenuinervis* |
| Confetti Tree | *Maytenus senegalensis* |
| Cork Bush | *Mundulea sericea* |
| Corky-Bark Monkey Orange | *Strychnos cocculoides* |
| Crystal-Bark | *Crossopteryx febrifuga* |
| Cups and Saucers | *Carphalea pubescens* |
| Diamond-Leaved Euclea | *Euclea divinorum* |
| Duikerberry | *Pseudolachnostylis maprouneifolia* |
| Fire-Thorned Rhus | *Rhus pyroides* |
| Glossy Combretum | *Combretum apiculatum* |
| Grey Grewia | *Grewia monticola* |
| Jasmine Pea | *Baphia massaiensis* |
| Knobby Bridelia | *Bridelia cathartica* |
| Large-Fruited Combretum | *Combretum zeyheri* |
| Large-Leaved Diospyros | *Diospyros kirkii* |
| Large-Leaved Euclea | *Euclea natalensis* |
| Live-Long | *Lannea discolor* |
| Long-Pod Cassia | *Cassia abbreviata* |
| Manketti Nut | *Schinziophyton rautanenii* |
| Monkeybread | *Piliostigma thonningii* |
| Mukwa | *Pterocarpus angolensis* |
| Munondo | *Julbernardia globiflora* |
| Musasa | *Brachystegia spiciformis* |
| Ordeal Tree | *Erythrophleum africanum* |
| Paperbark Acacia | *Acacia sieberiana* |
| Paperbark Albizia | *Albizia tanganyicensis* |
| Paperbark Commiphora | *Commiphora marlothii* |

| Tree/Shrub Name | Botanical Name |
|---|---|
| Peeling-Bark Ochna | *Ochna pulchra* |
| Poison-Grub Commiphora | *Commiphora africana* |
| Prince-of-Wales Feathers | *Brachystegia boehmii* |
| Rigid Star-Berry | *Diospyros squarrosa* |
| River Rhus | *Rhus quartiniana* |
| Rough-Leaved Commiphora | *Commiphora edulis* |
| Round-Leaved Bloodwood | *Pterocarpus rotundifolius* |
| Scented-Pod Acacia | *Acacia nilotica* |
| Scotsman's Rattle | *Amblygonocarpus andongensis* |
| Shaving-Brush Combretum | *Combretum mossambicense* |
| Shiny Fruited Rhus | *Rhus lucens* |
| Shiny-leaved Mukwakwa | *Strychnos madagascariensis* |
| Single-Leaved Commiphora | *Commiphora glandulosa* |
| Small Sourplum | *Ximenia americana* |
| Sycomore Fig | *Ficus sycomorus* |
| Tick Tree | *Sterculia africana* |
| Umtshibi | *Guibourtia coleosperma* |
| Waterberry | *Syzygium cordatum* |
| White Bauhinia | *Bauhinia petersiana* |
| Wild Medlar | *Vangueria infausta* |
| Wild Rubber | *Diplorhynchus condylocarpon* |
| Wild Wisteria | *Bolusanthus speciosus* |
| Zambezi Teak | *Baikiaea plurijuga* |

## INTO AFRICA TRAVEL GUIDES

Bvumba: Magic in the Mist

Hwange: Elephant Country

Kariba: Nyaminyami's Kingdom

Great Zimbabwe: Houses of Stone

Victoria Falls: Mosi-oa-Tunya

Serengeti: Endless Plains

Ngorongoro: The Eighth Wonder

Kilimanjaro: African Beacon

Zanzibar: Spice Islands

# INDEX